Gleaming Mandala

Copyright: Published in the United States by Tamara Loehr
Published December 2016
ISBN-13: 978-1541270299
ISBN-10: 1541270290

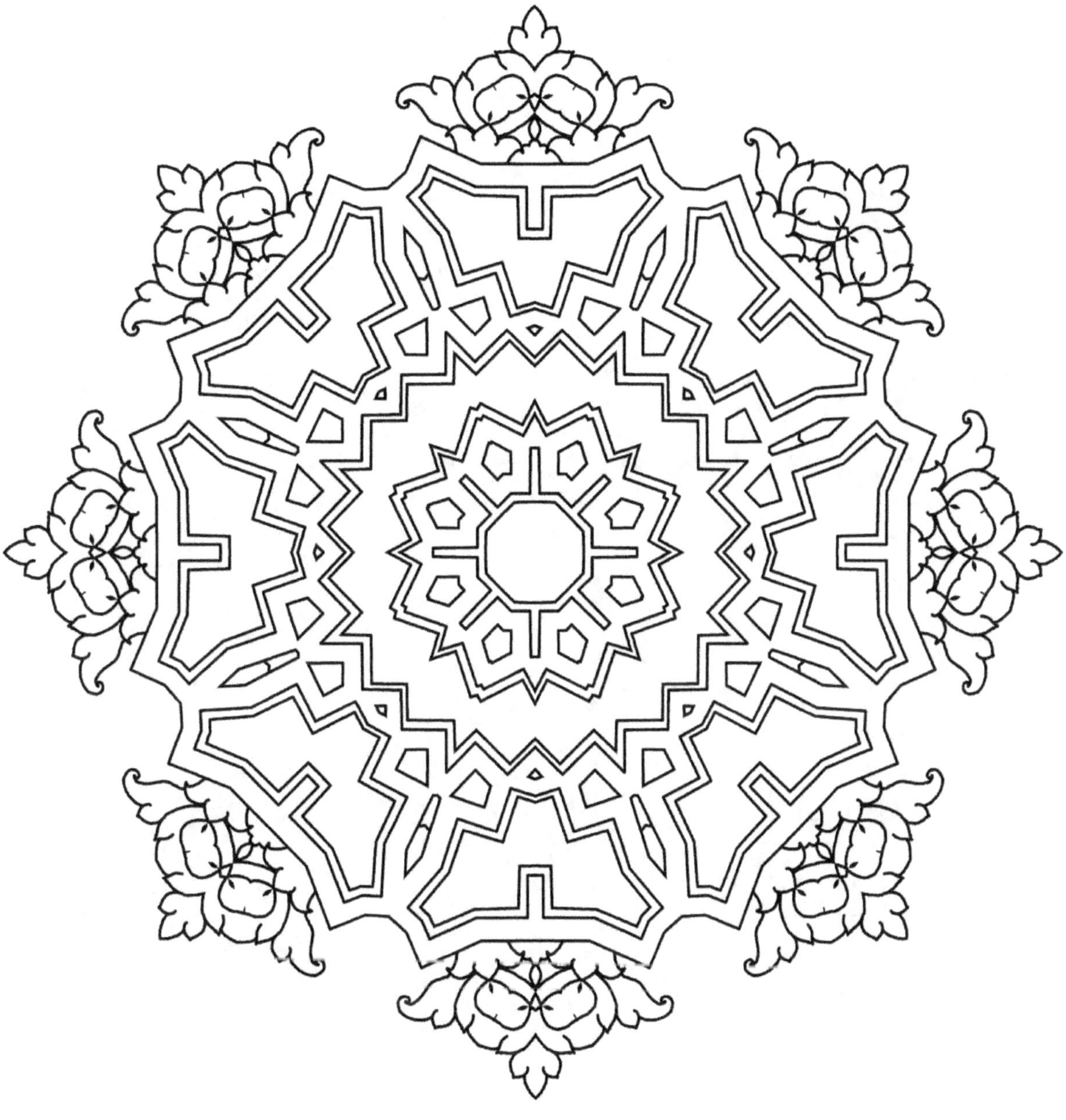

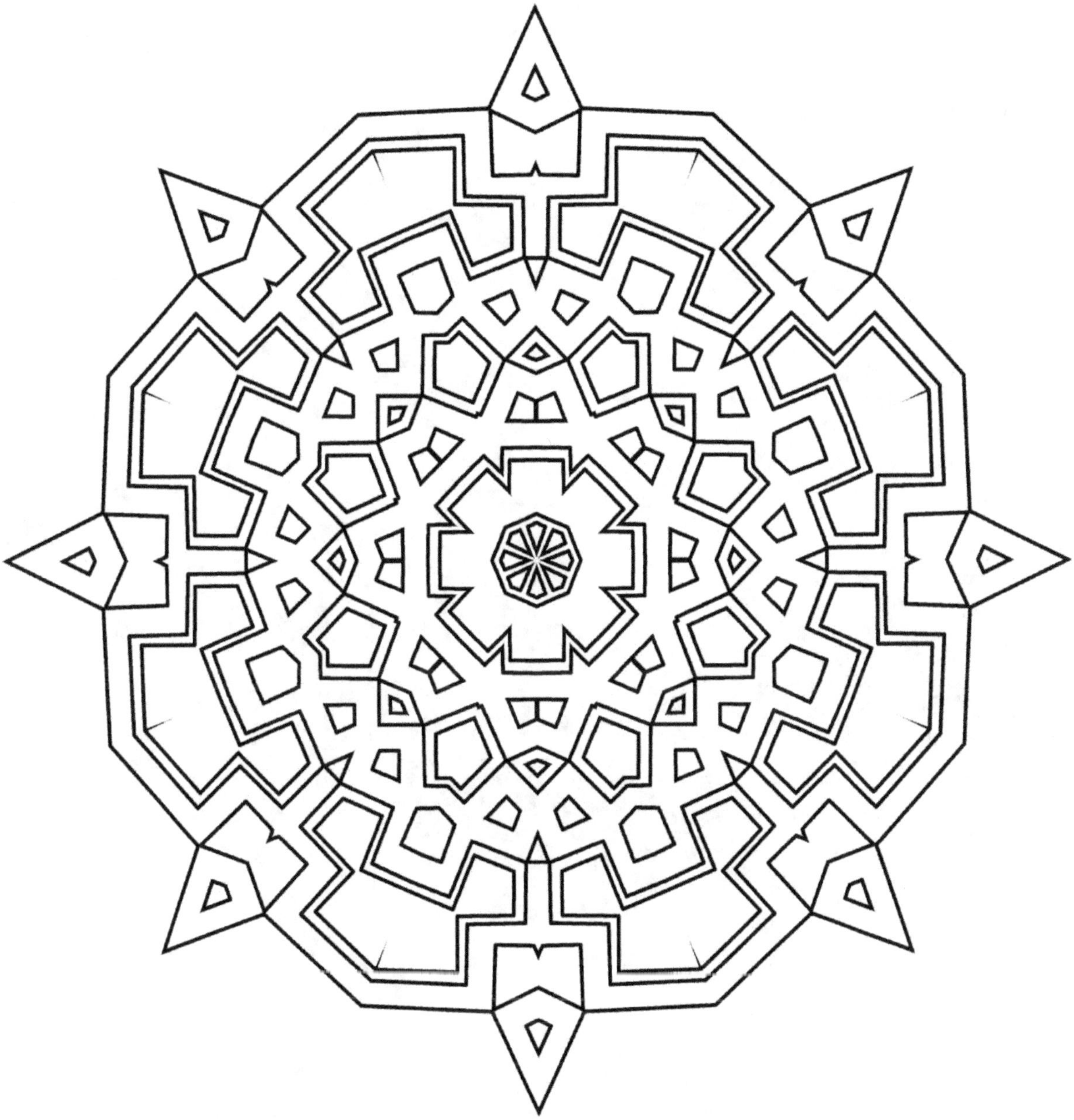

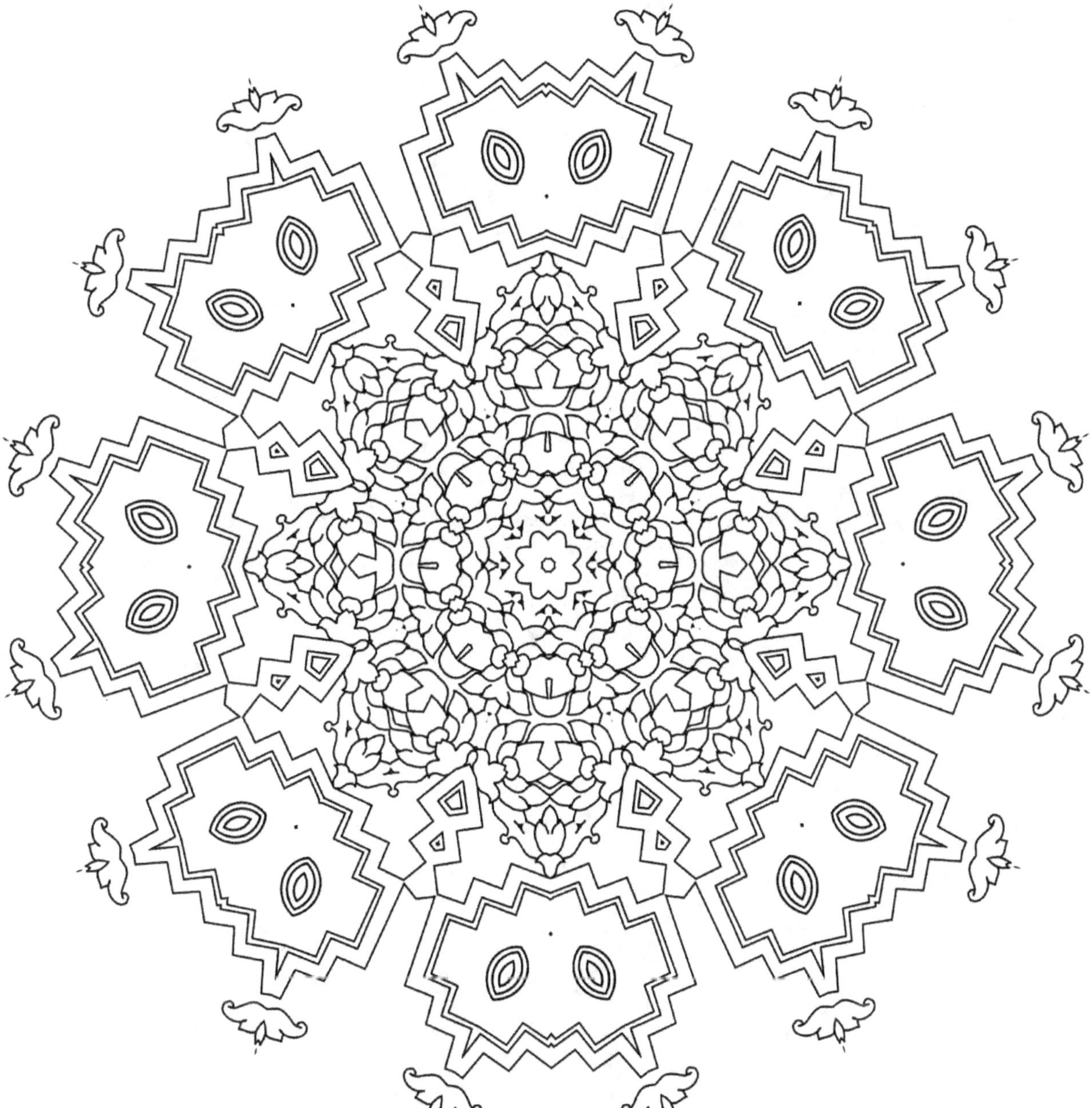

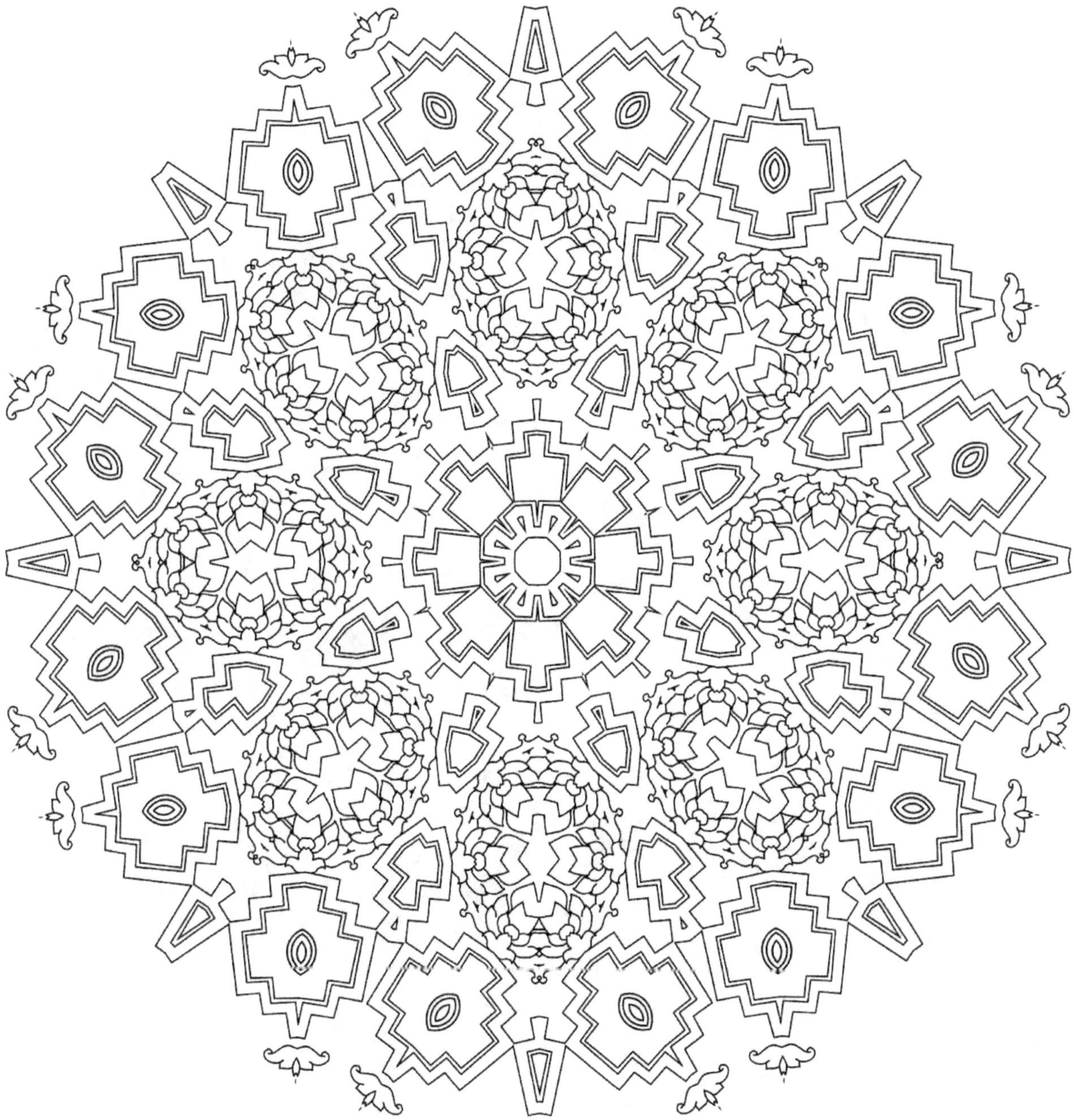

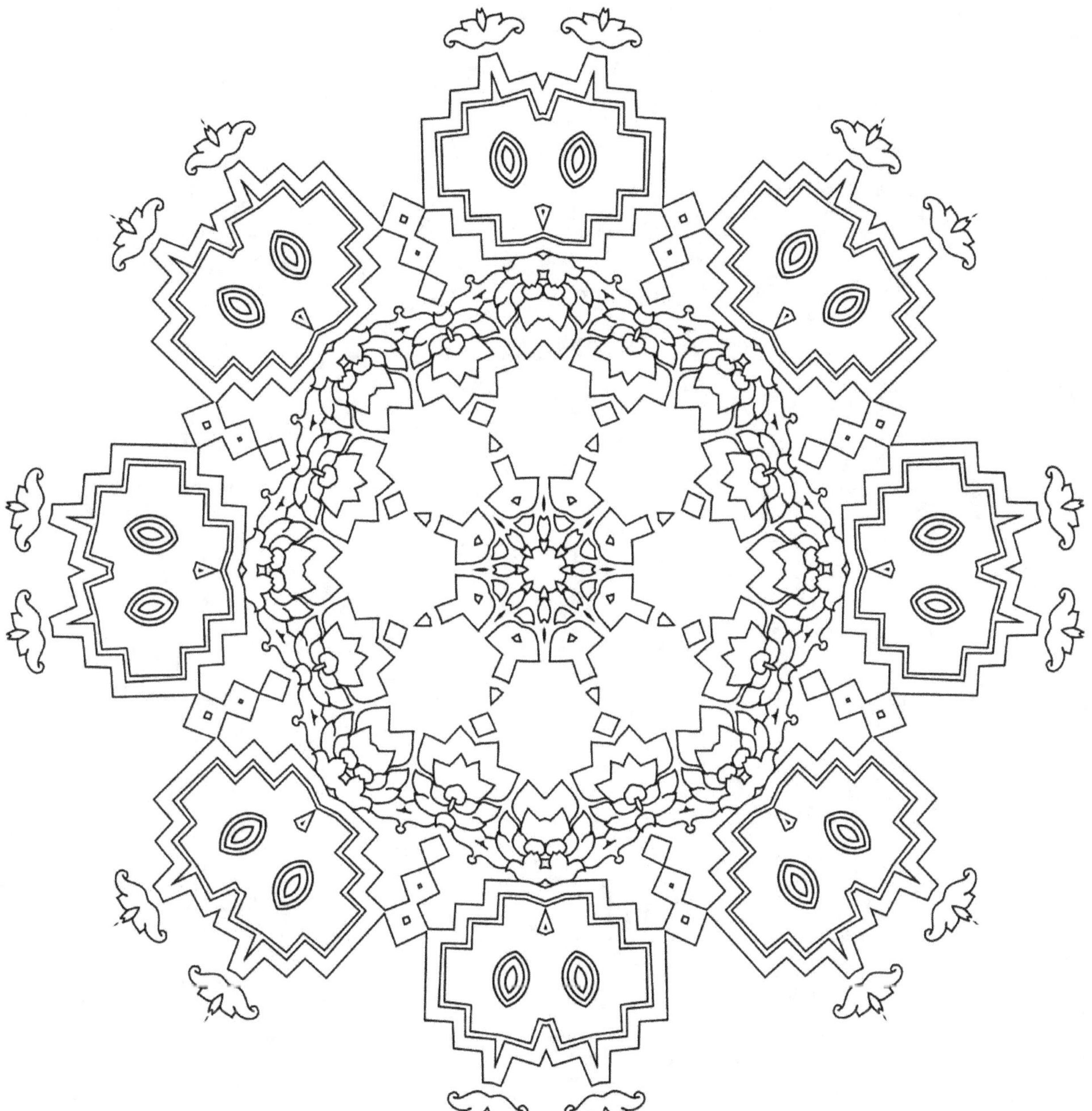

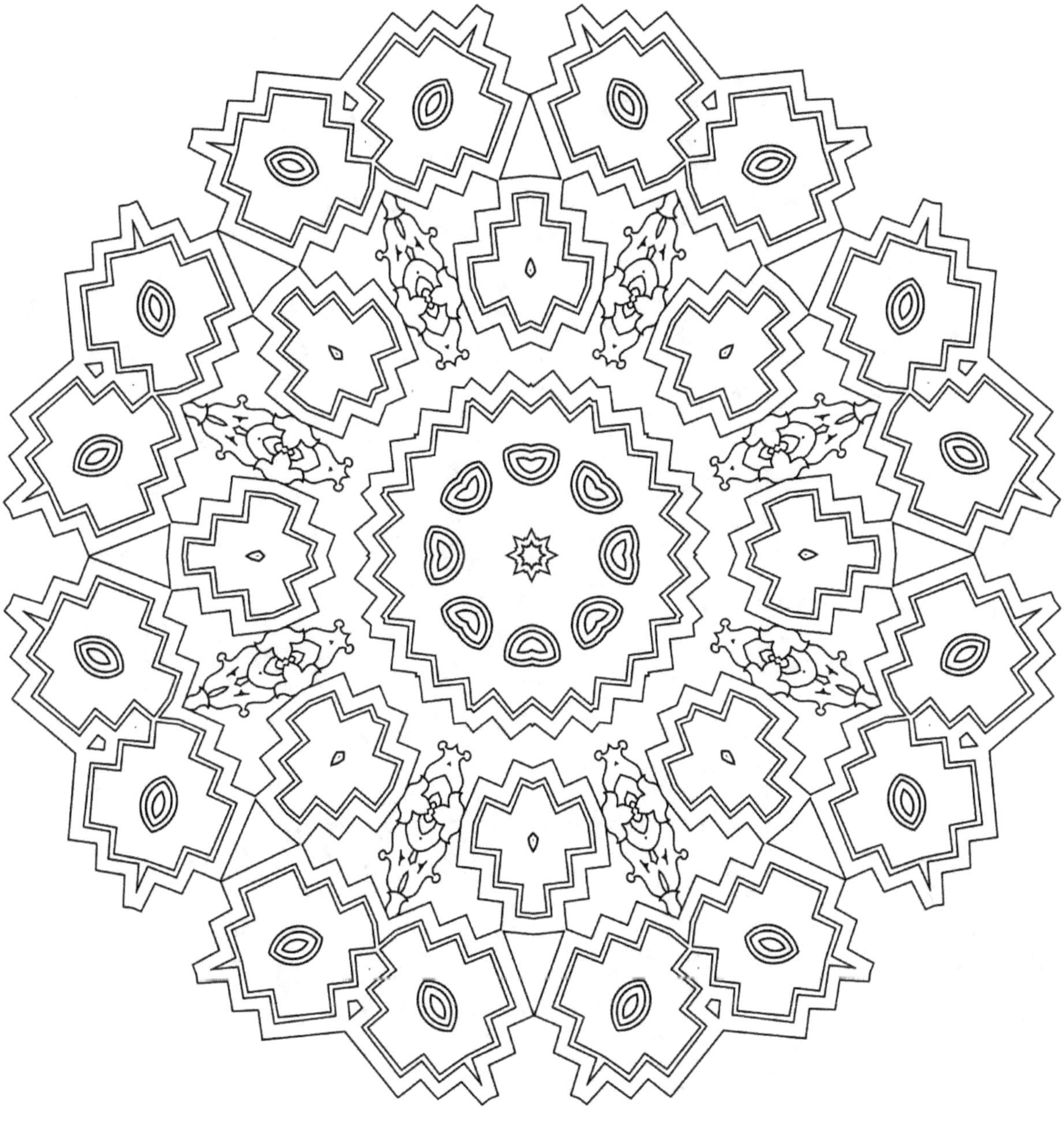

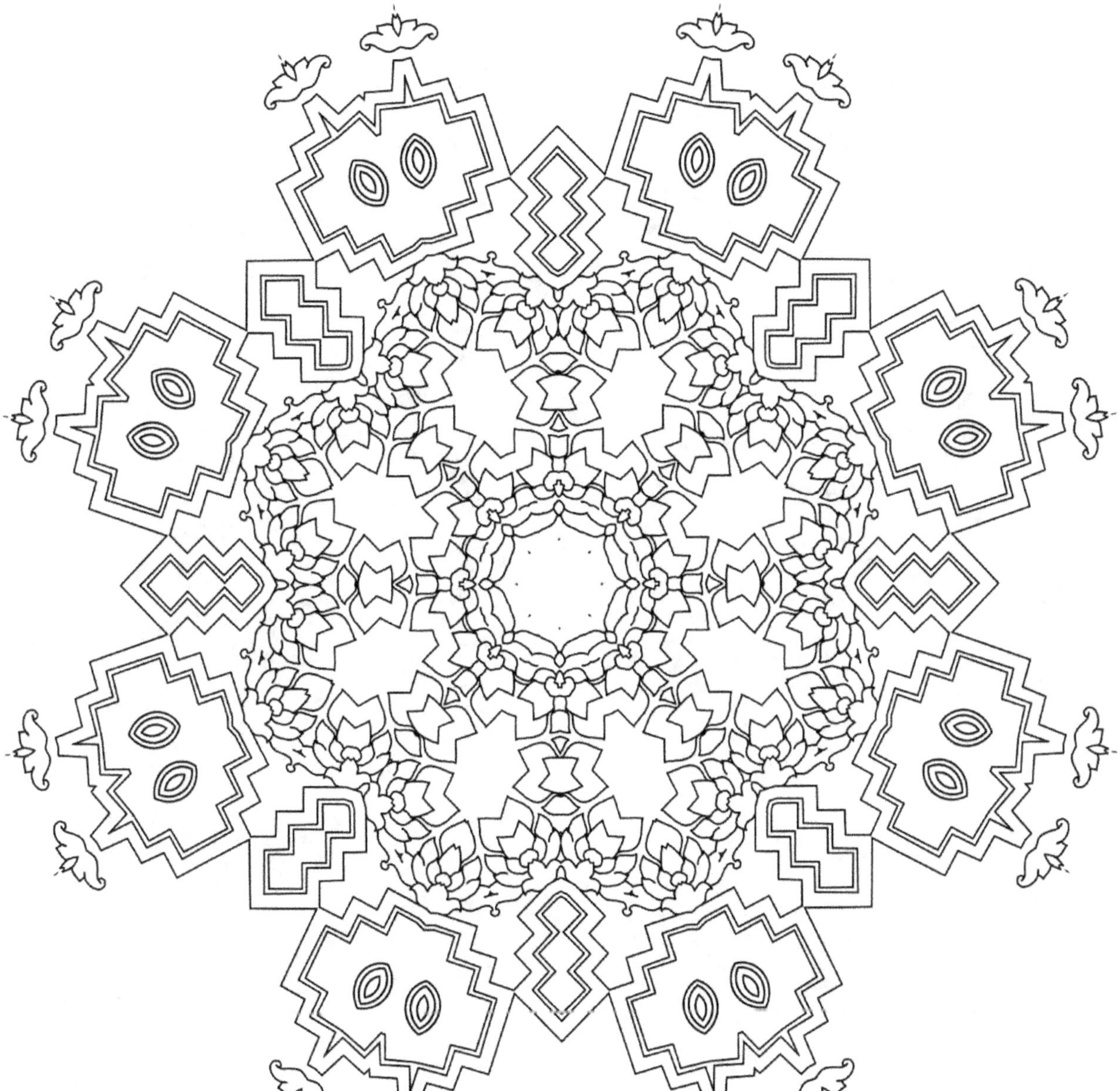

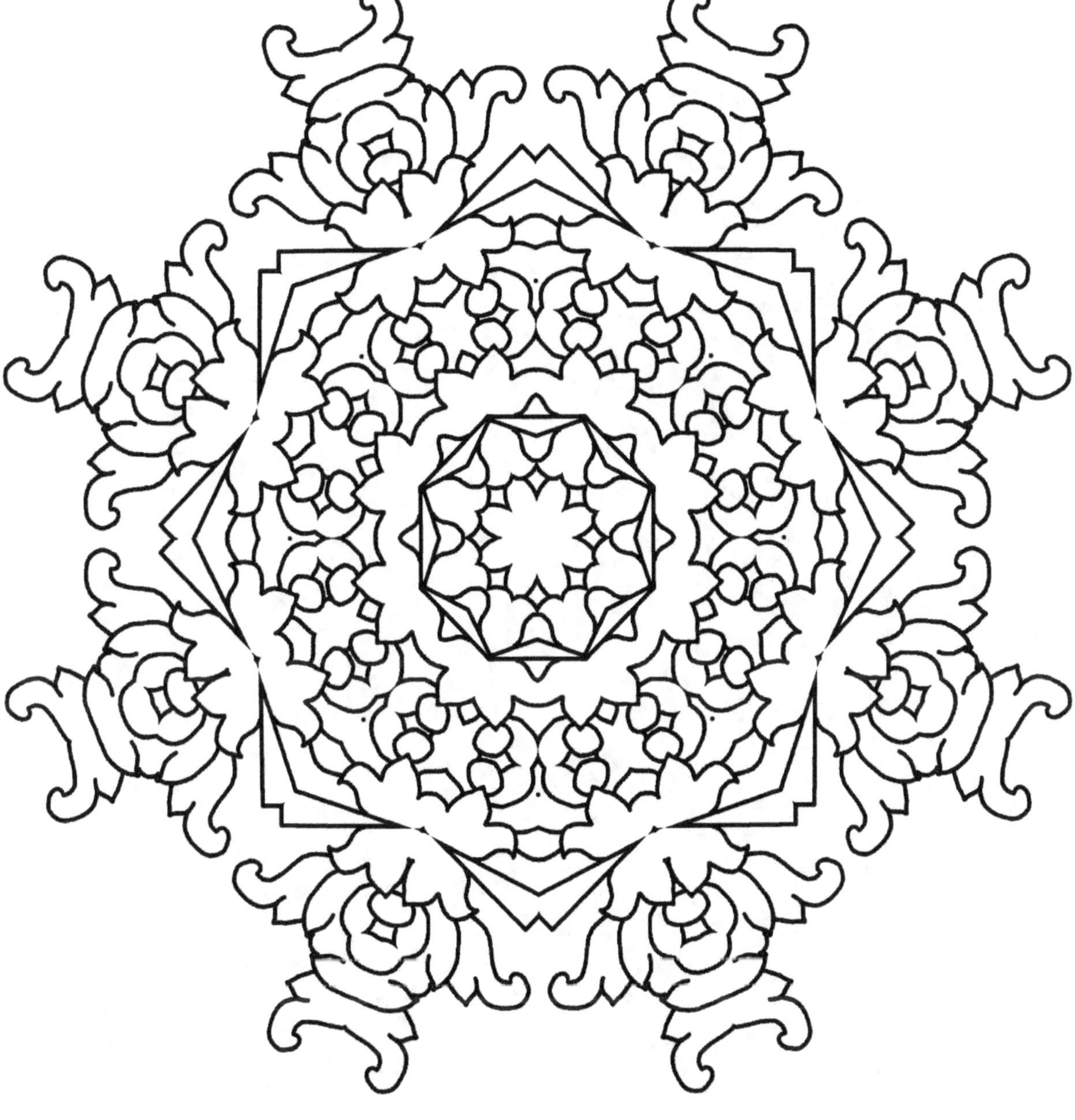

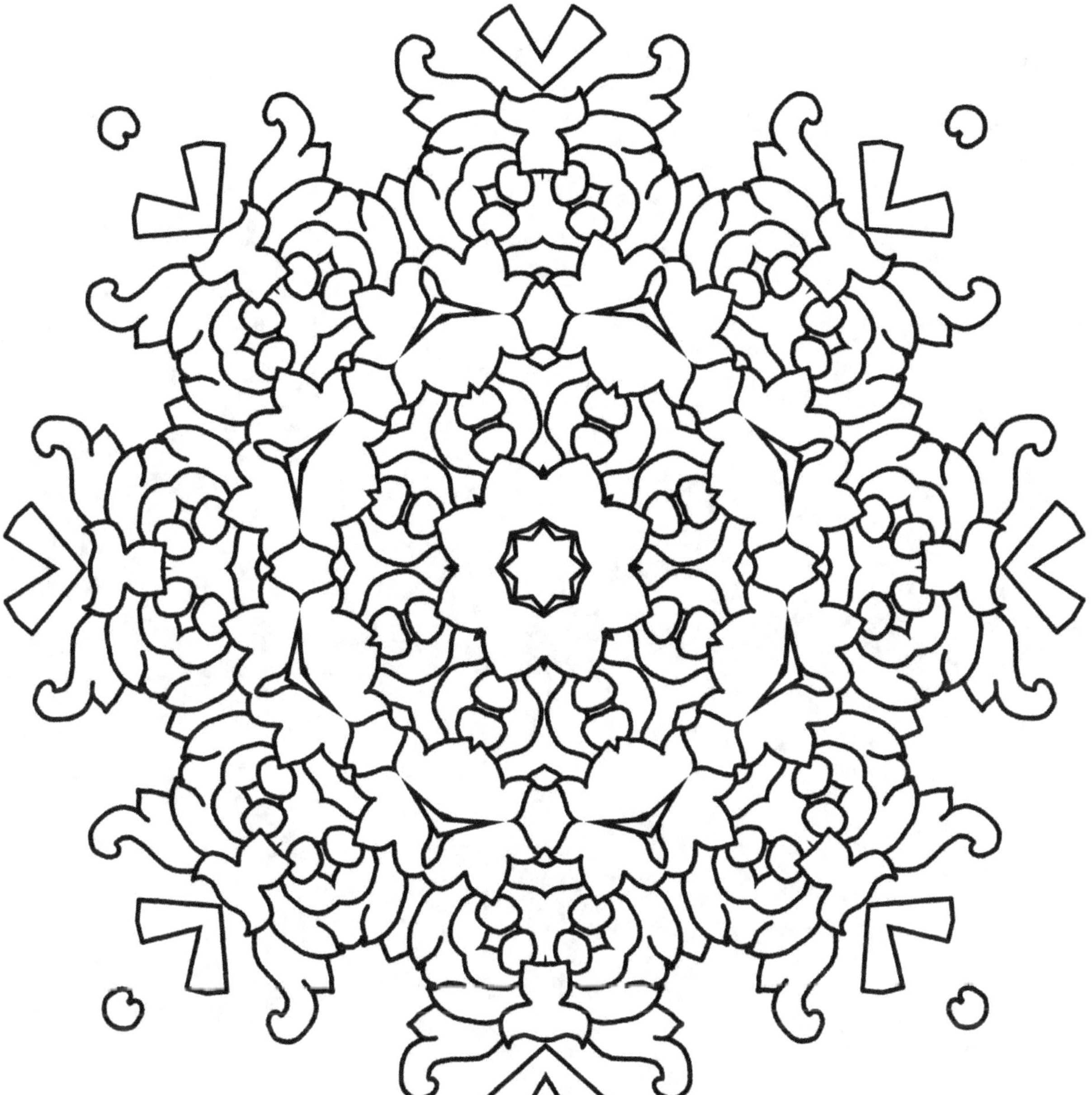

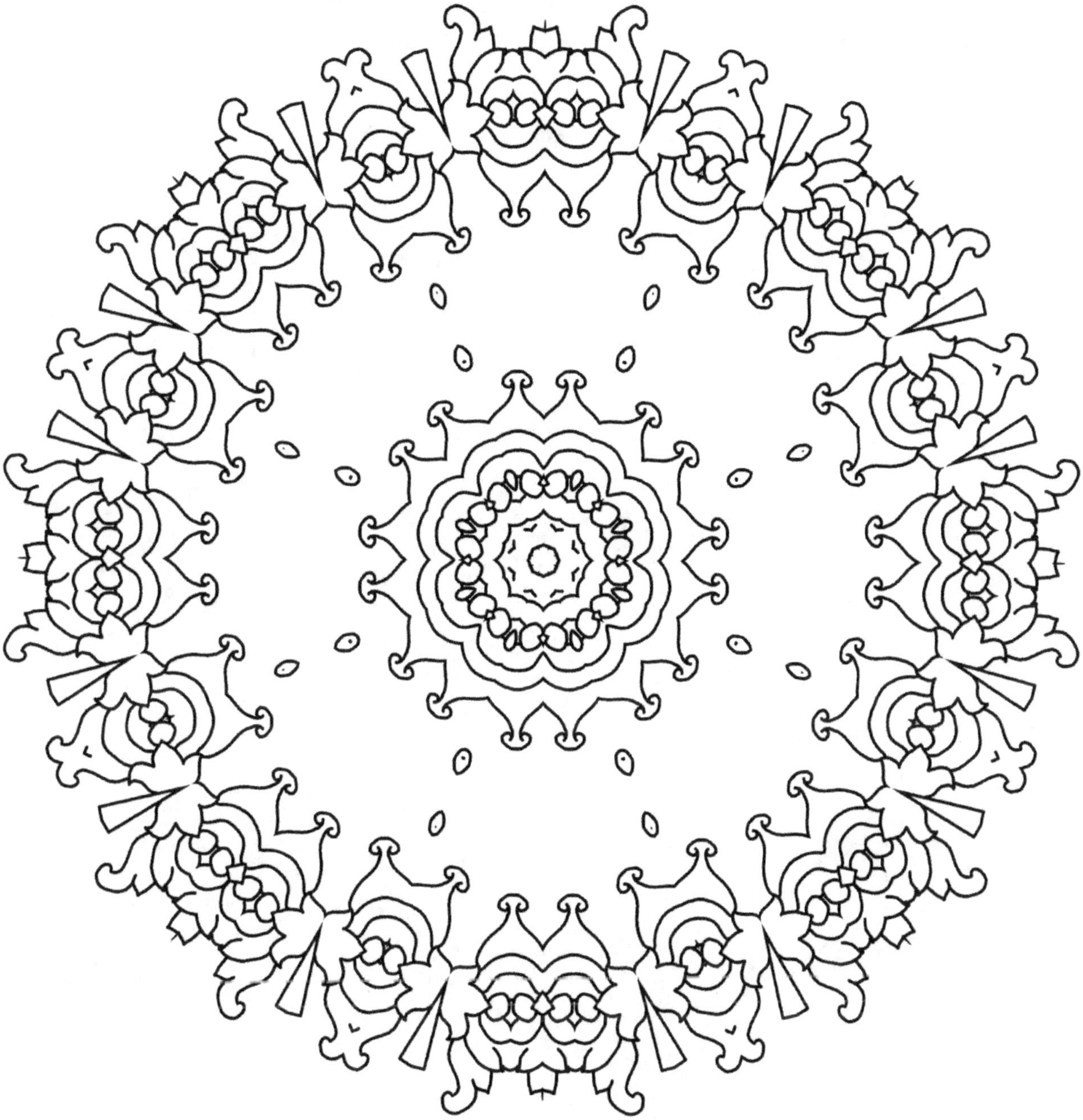

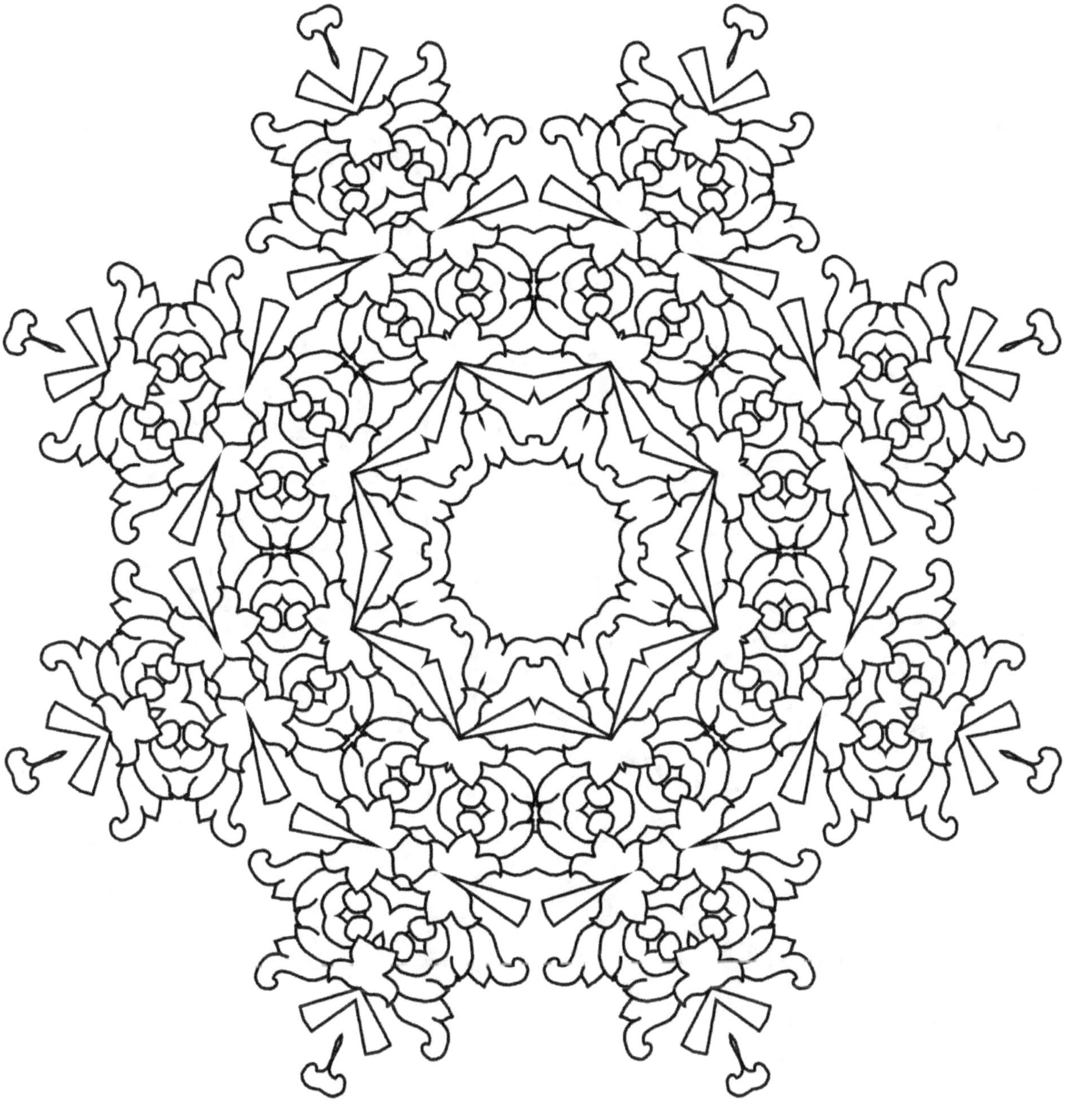

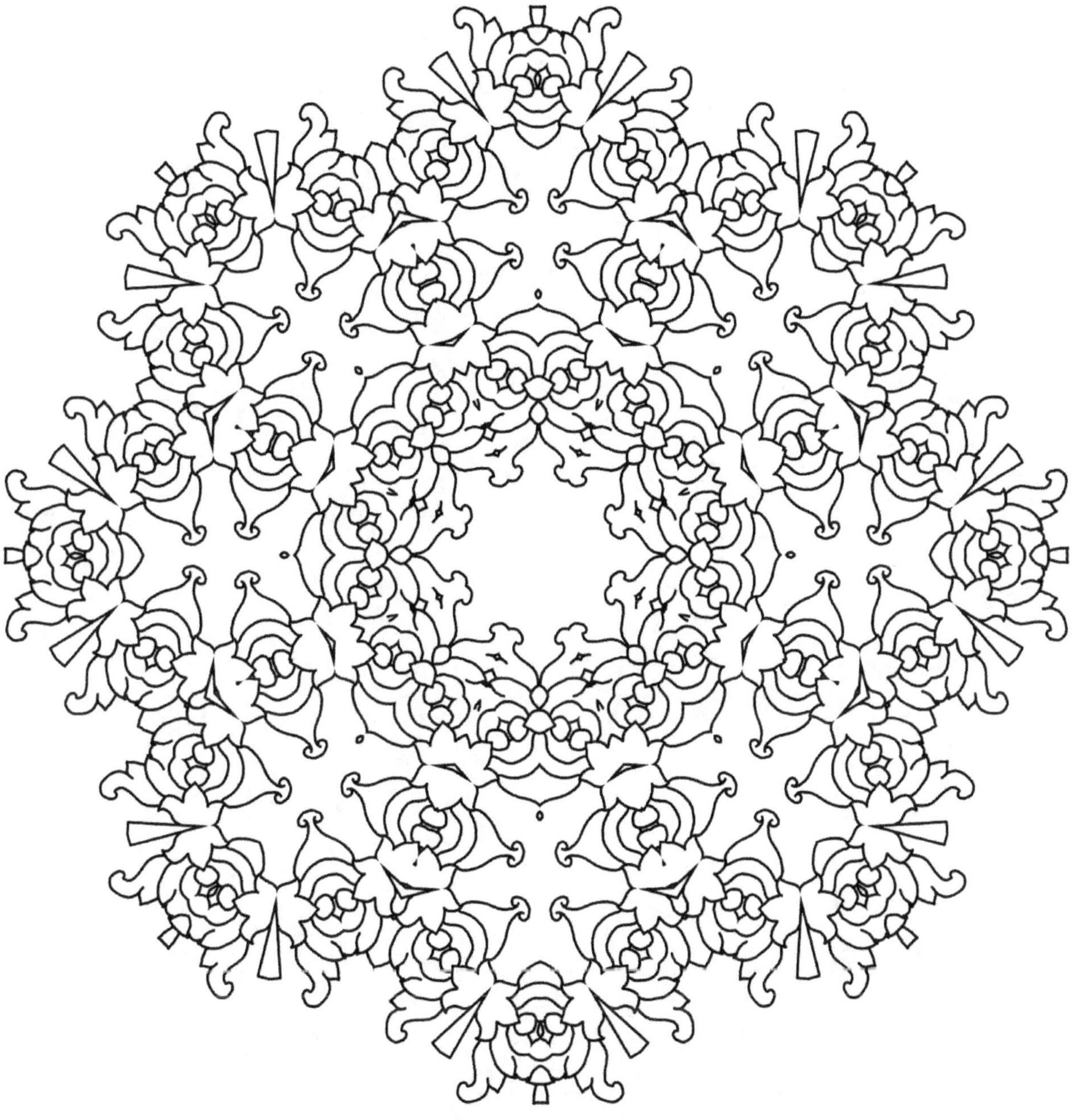

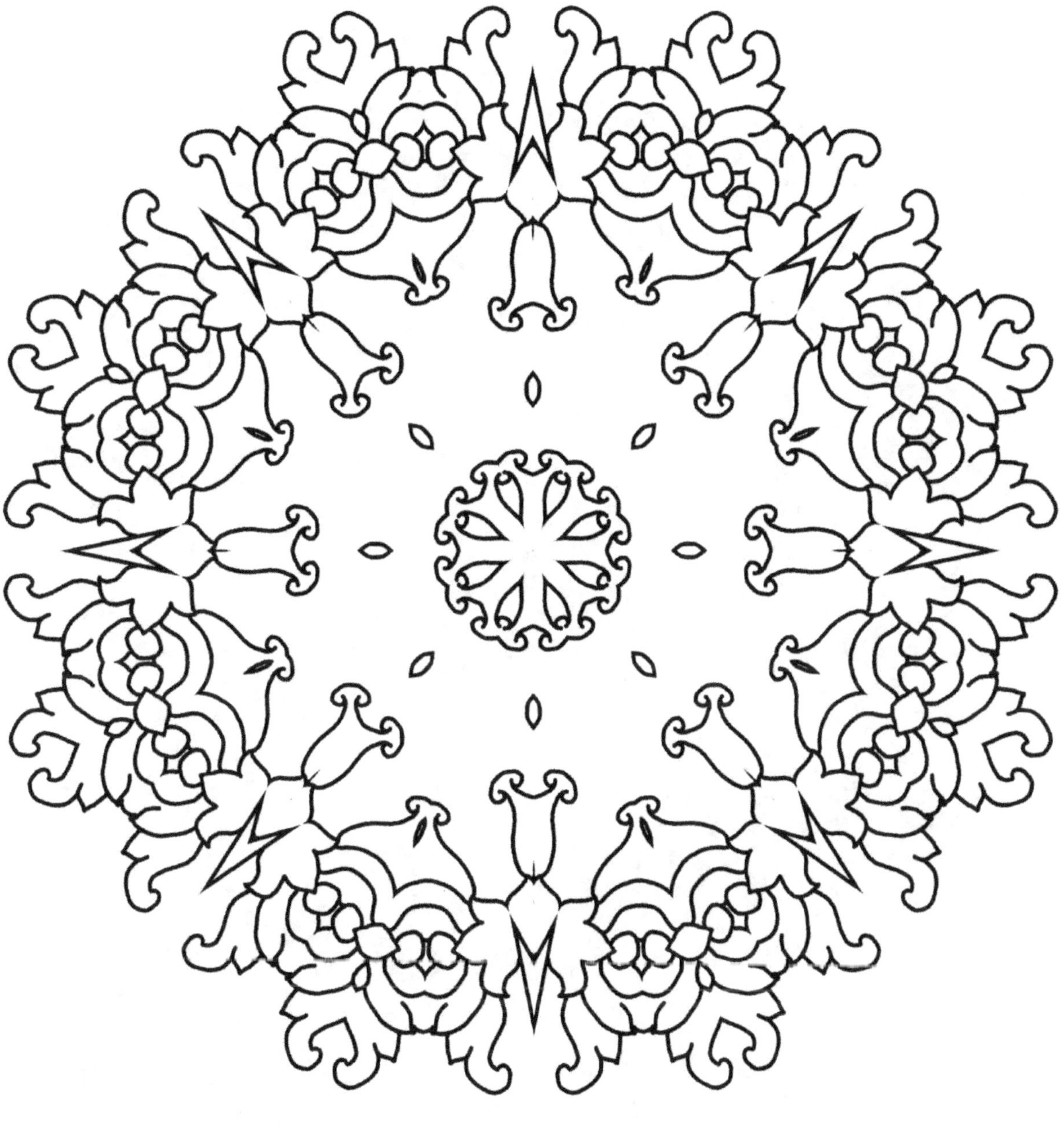

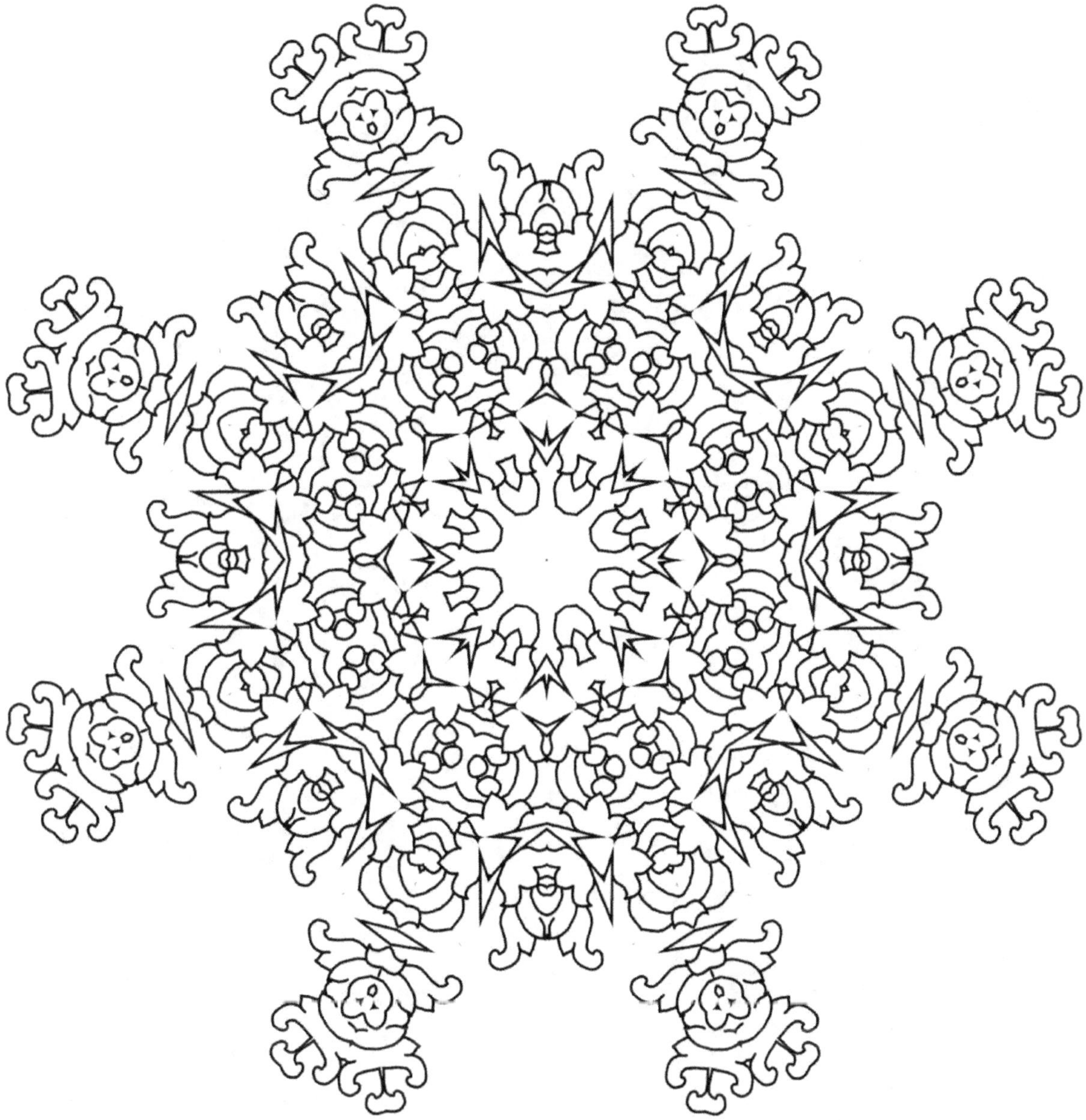

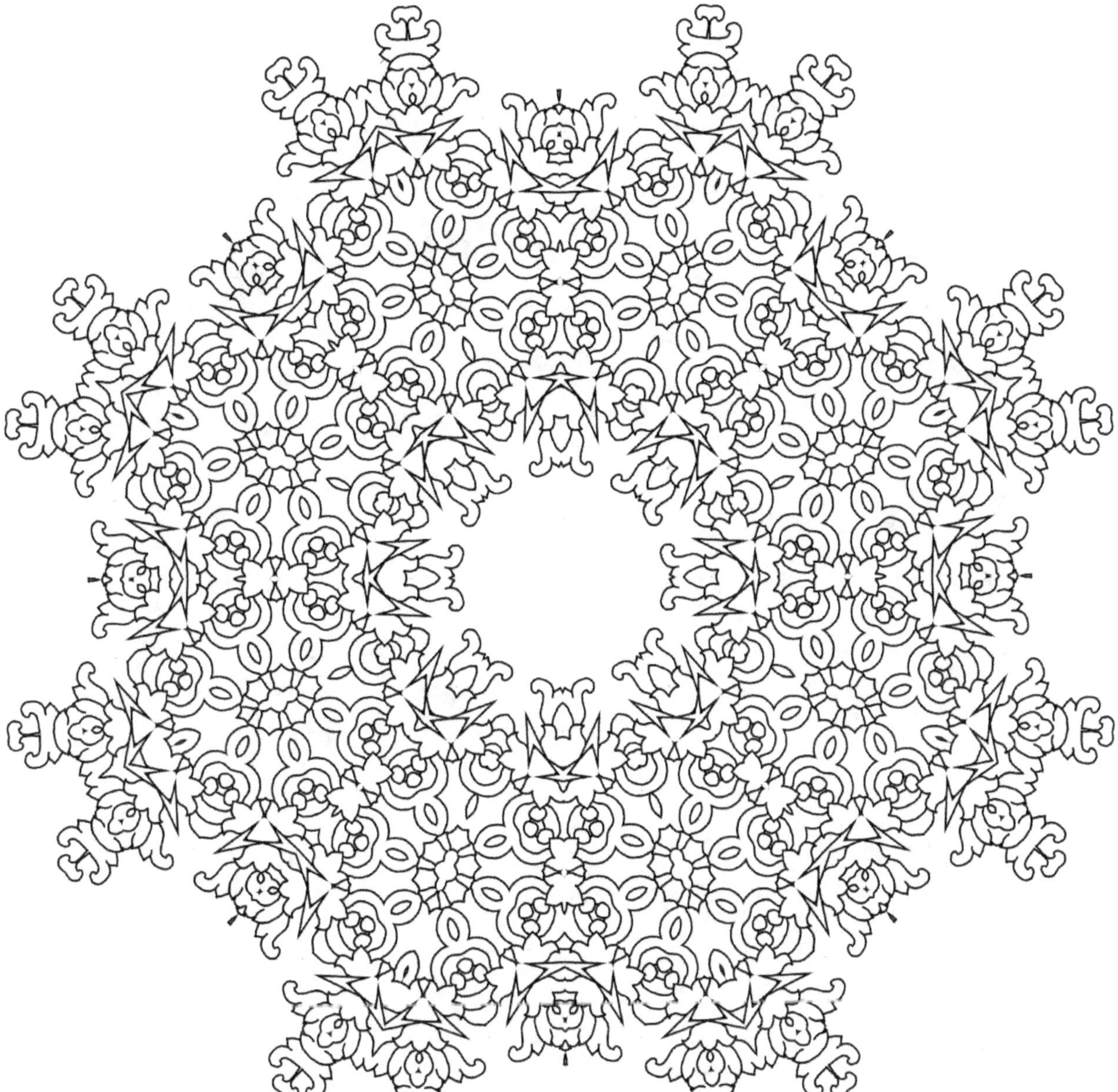

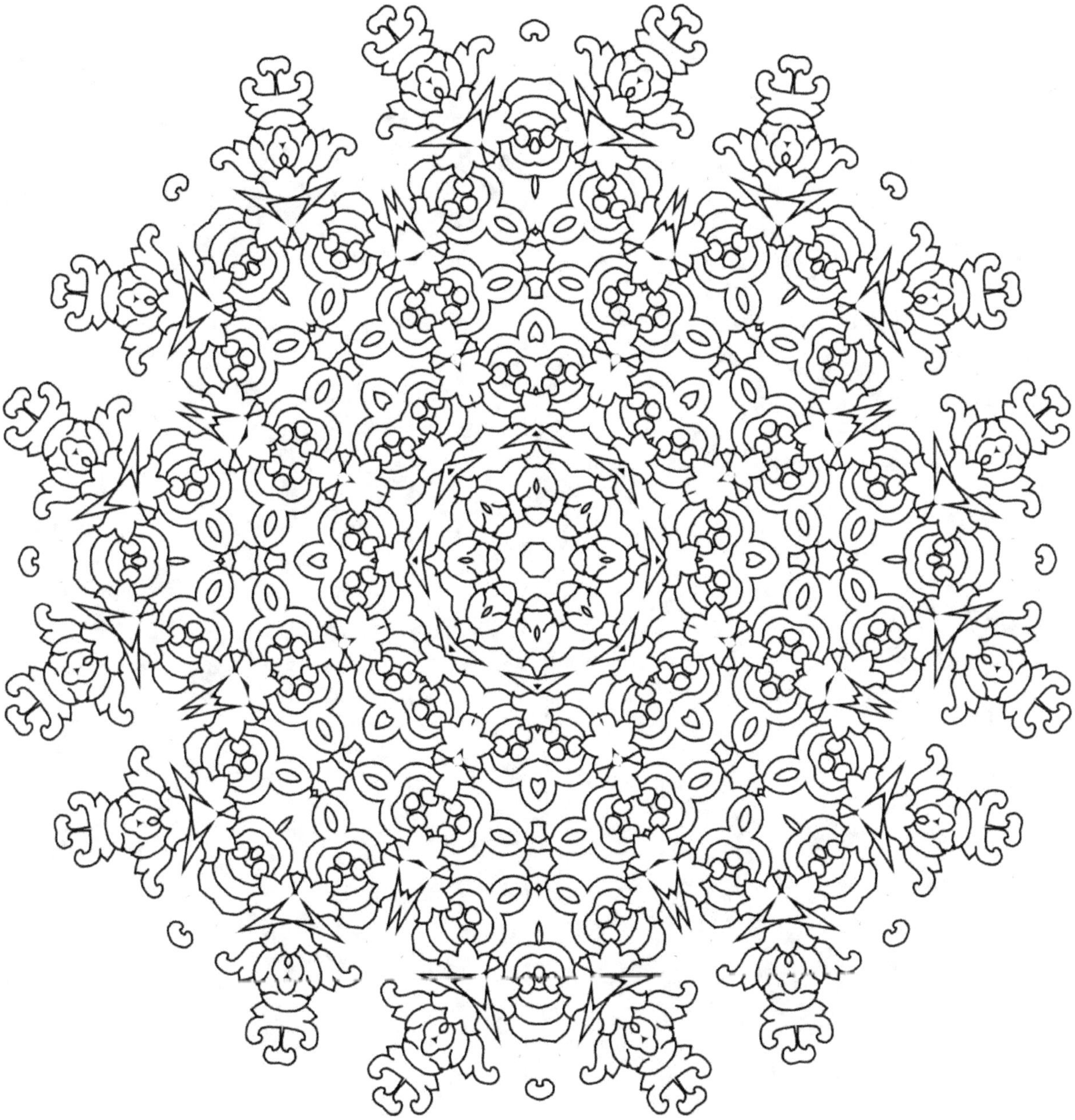

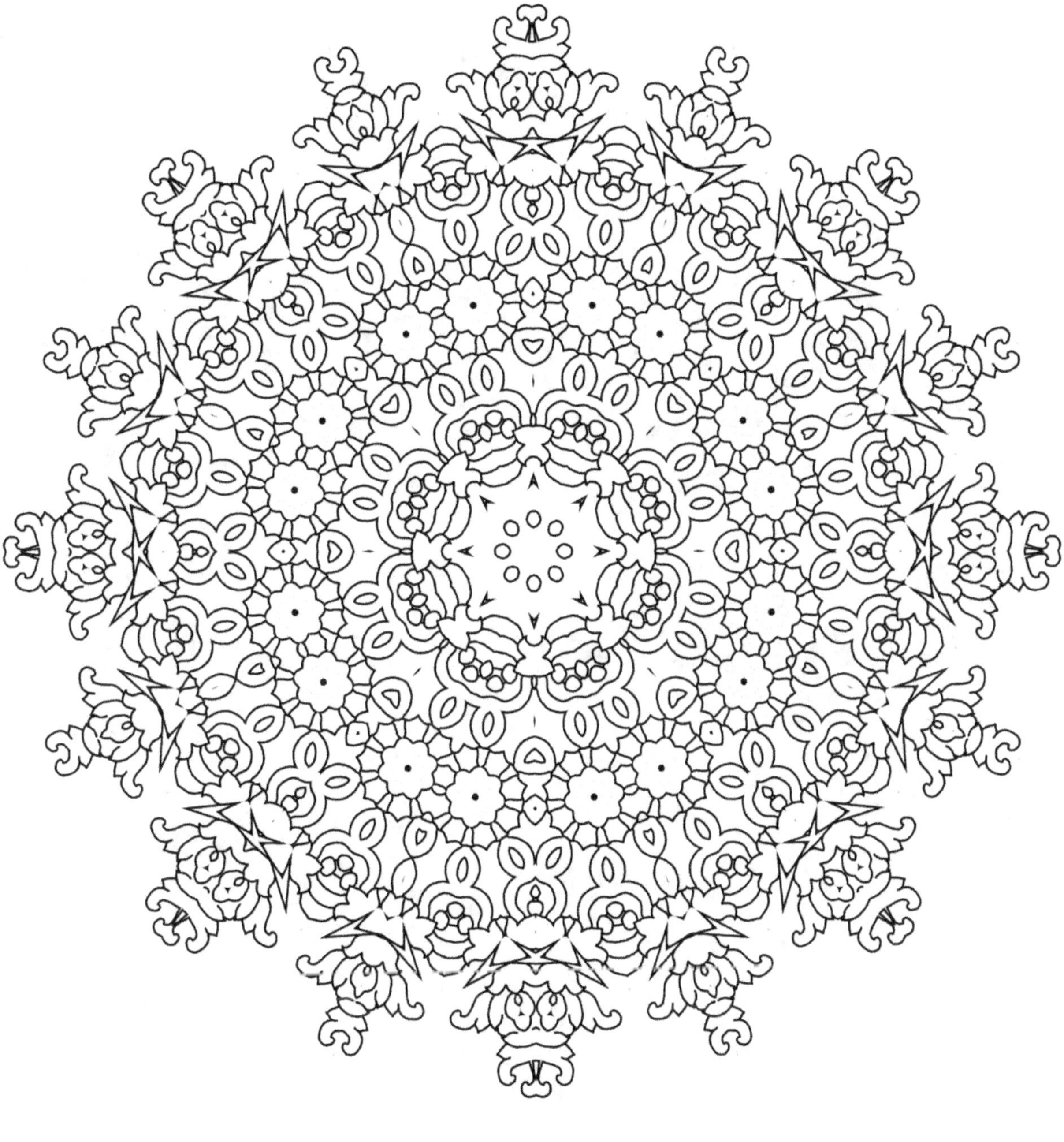

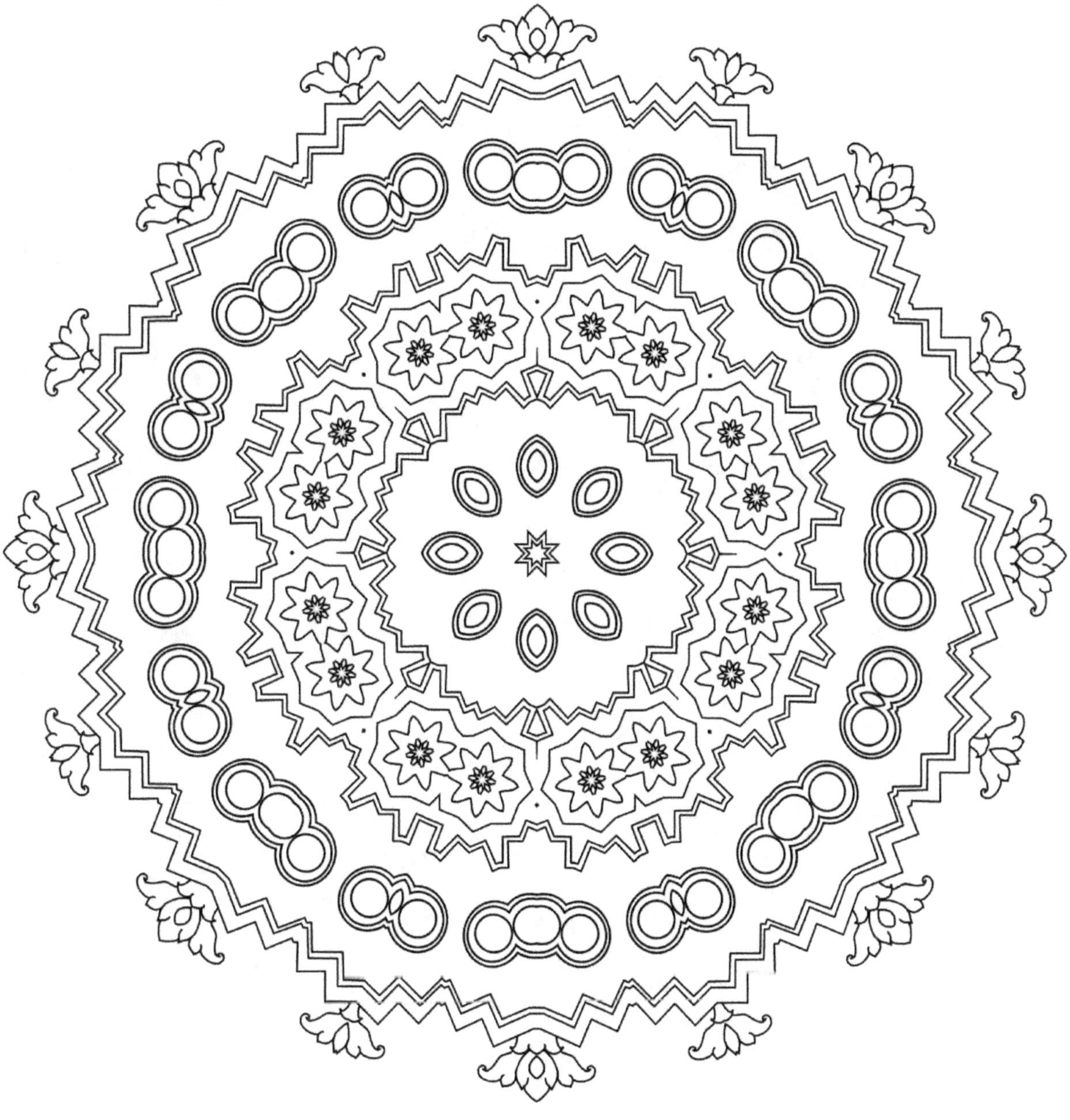

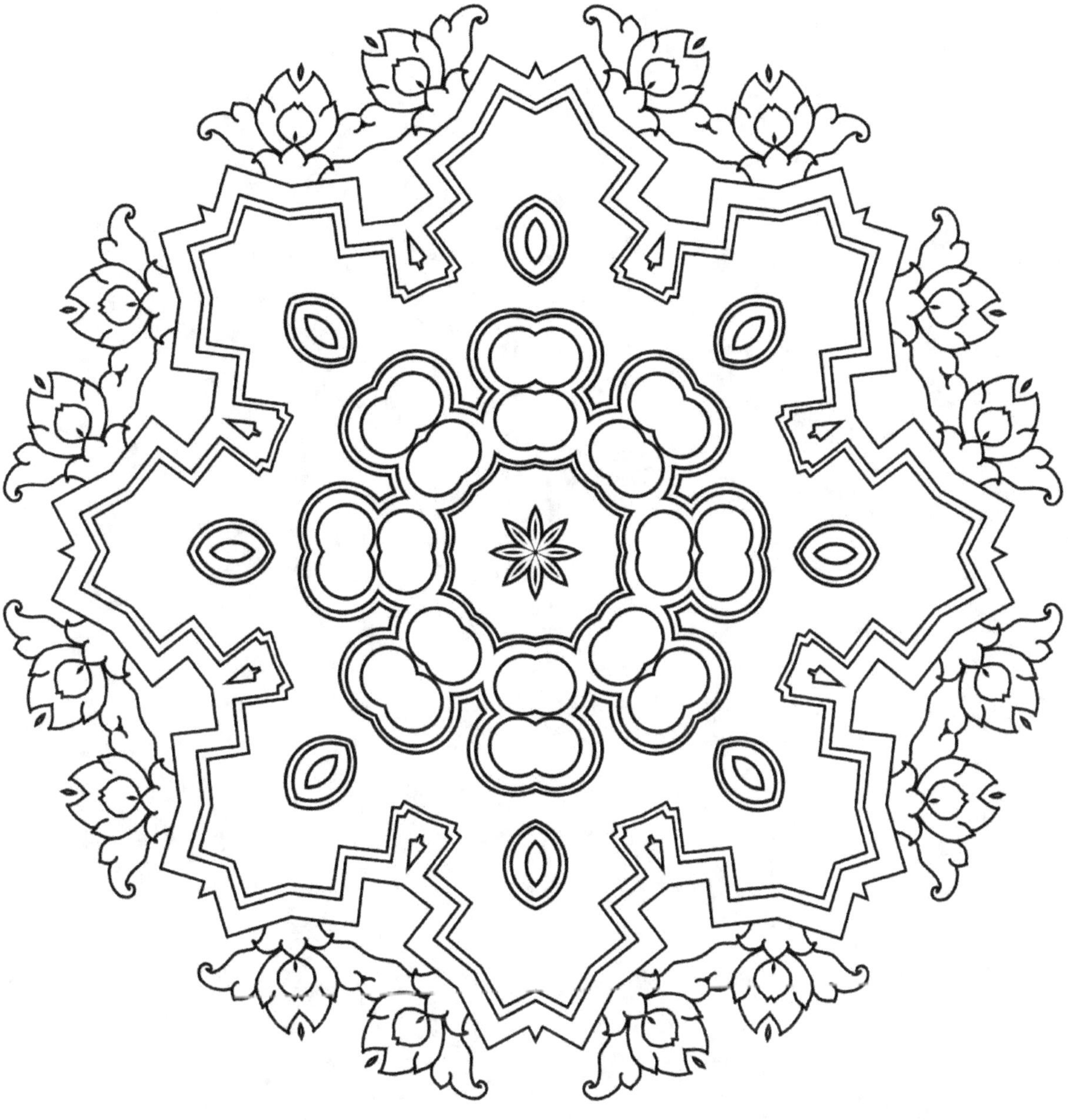

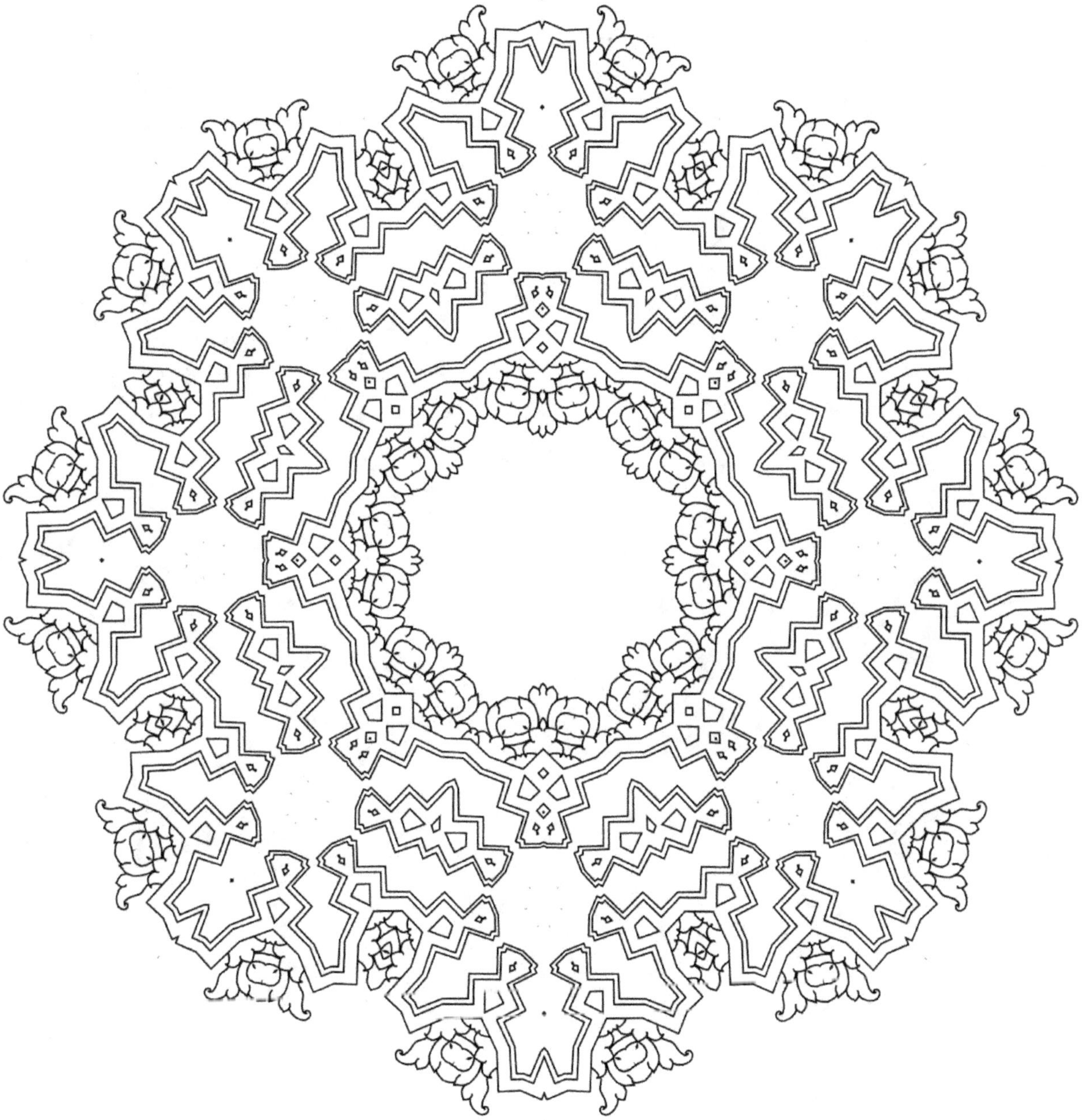

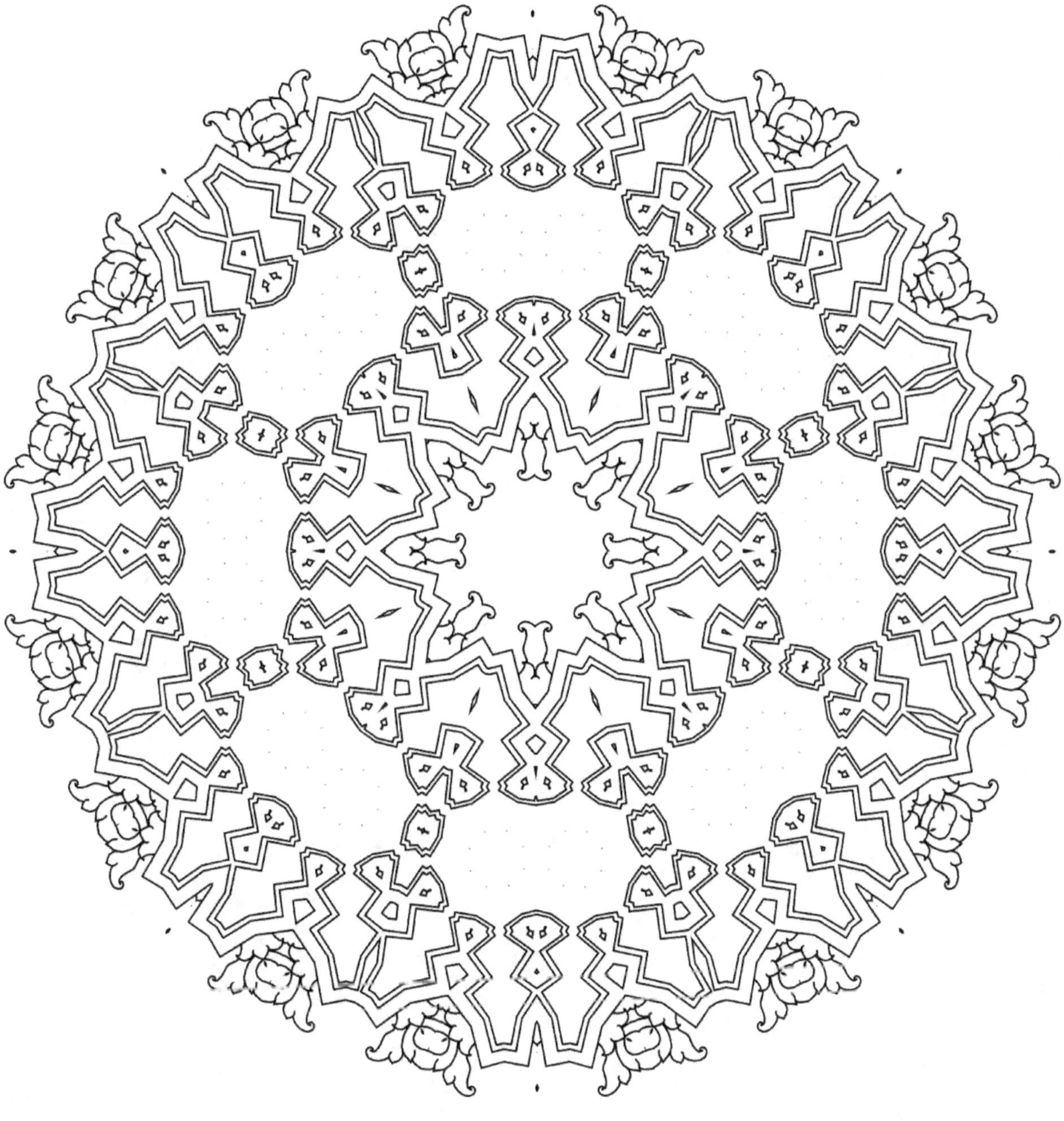

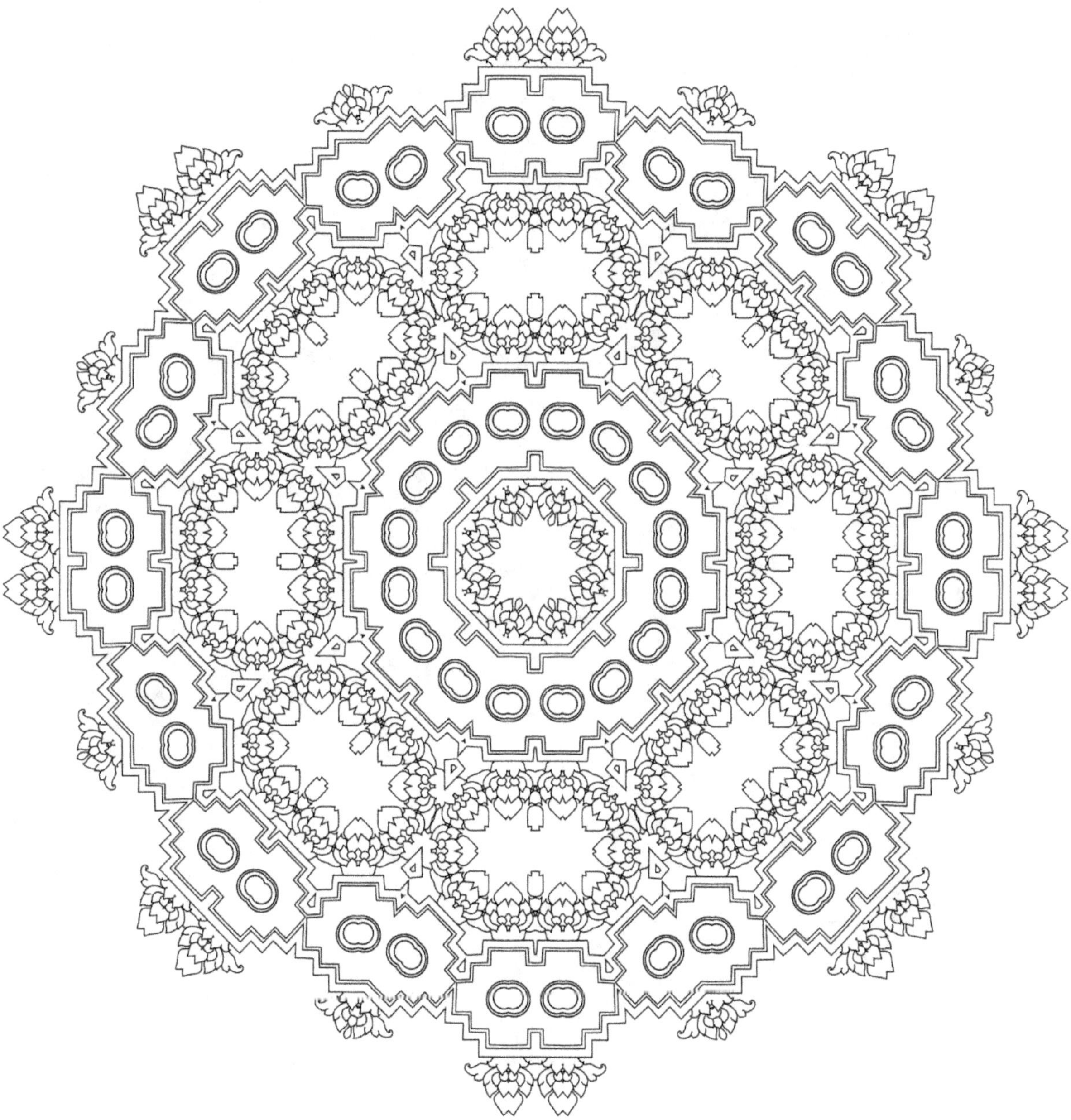

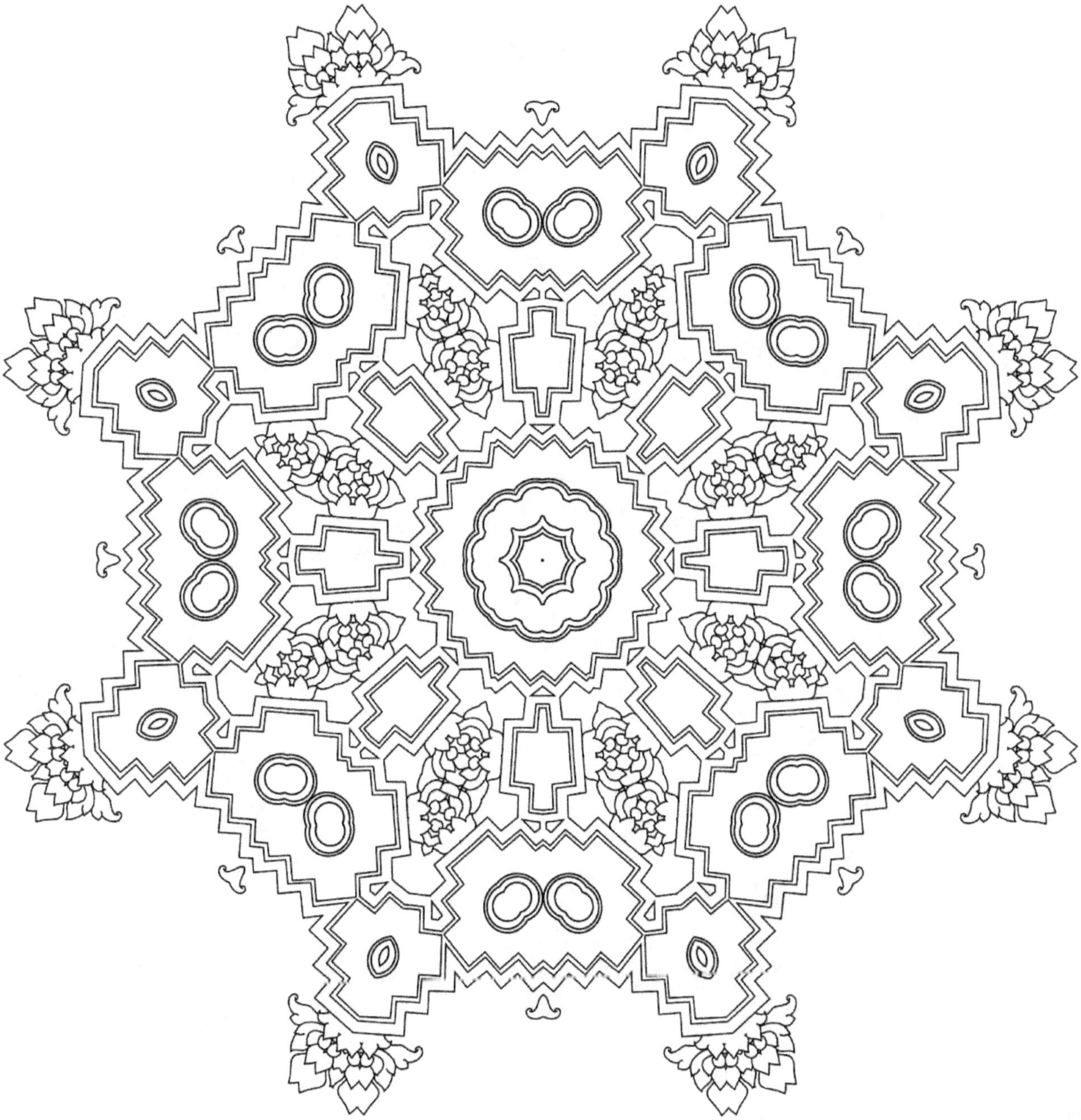

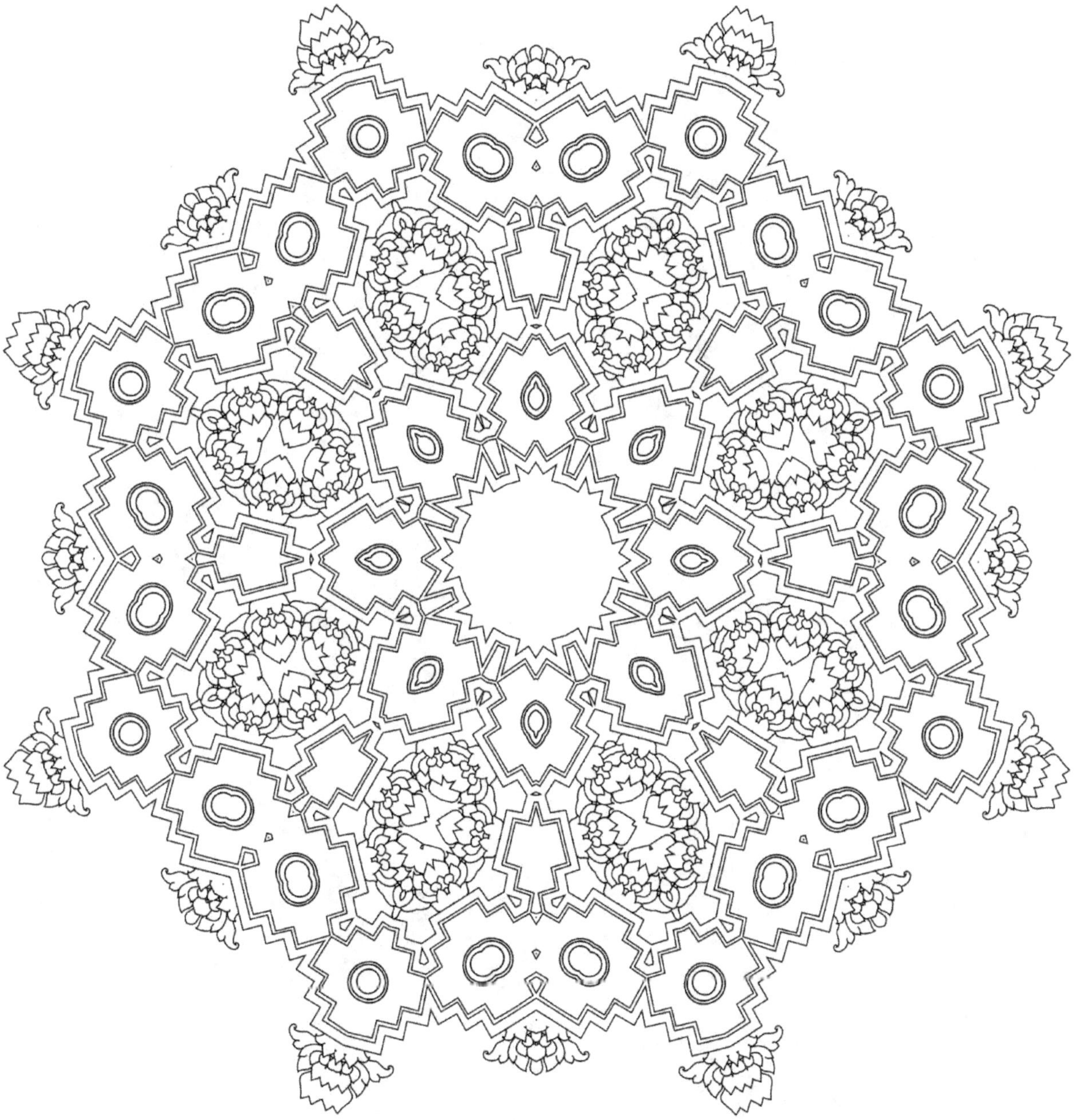

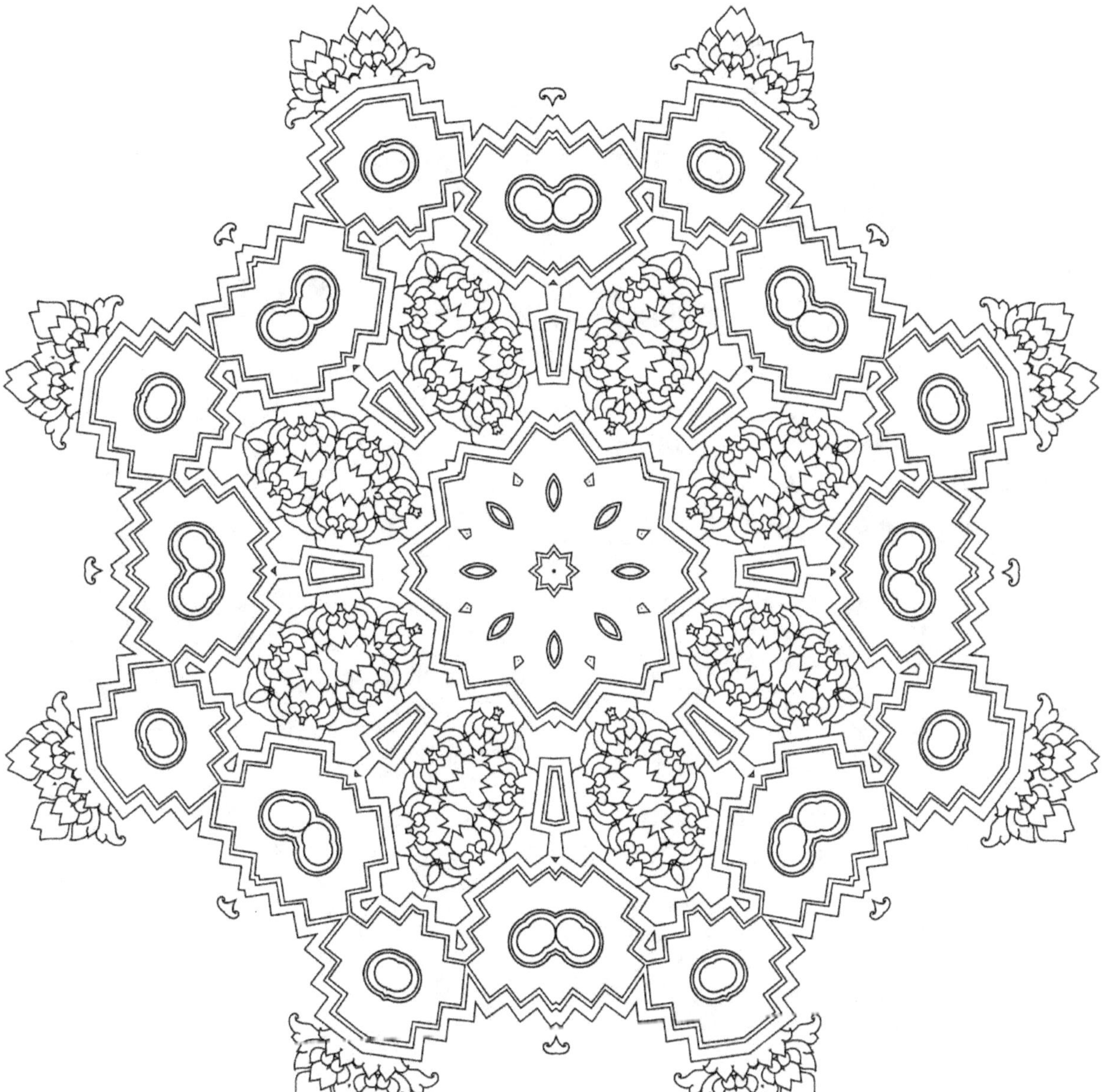

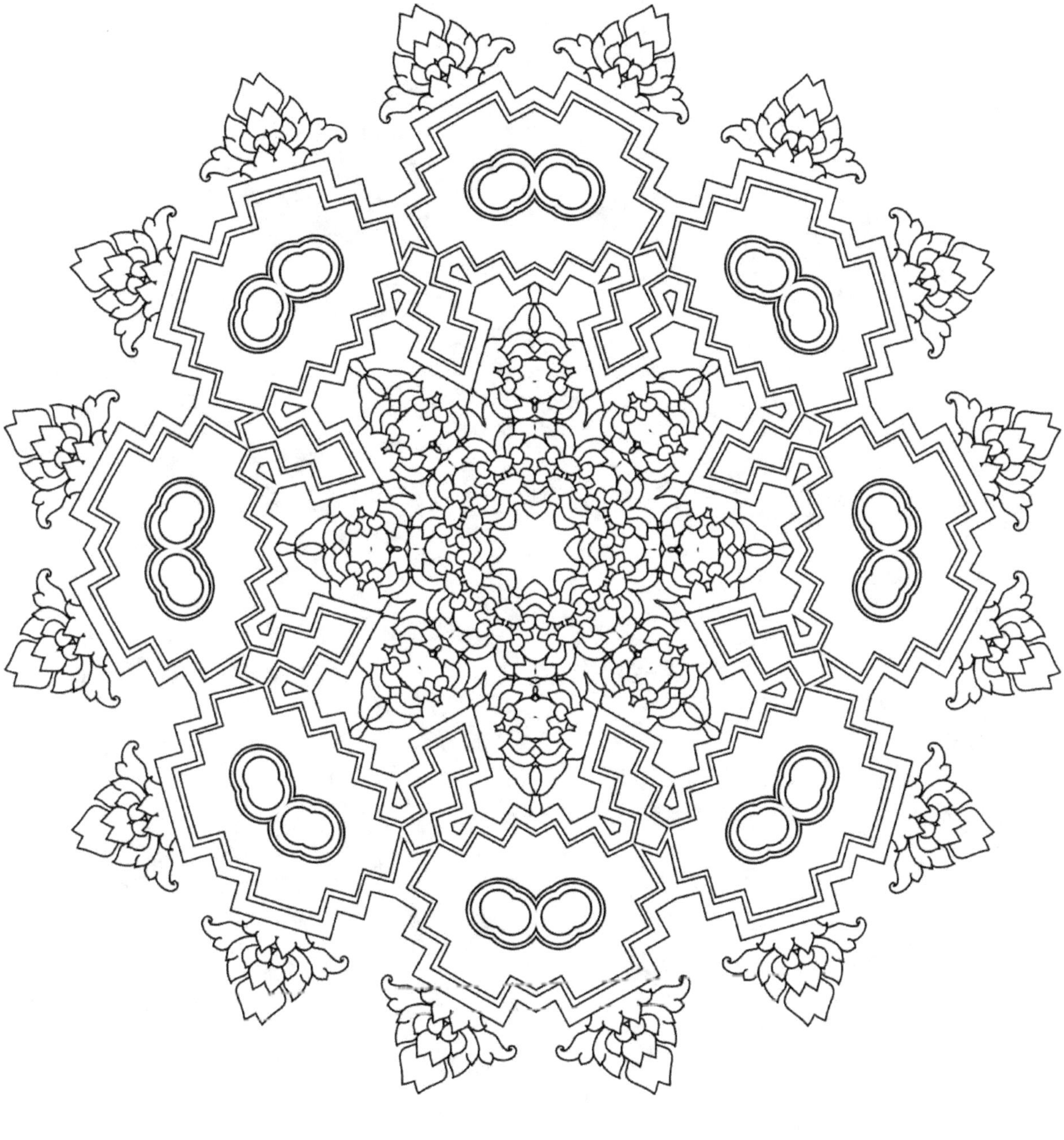

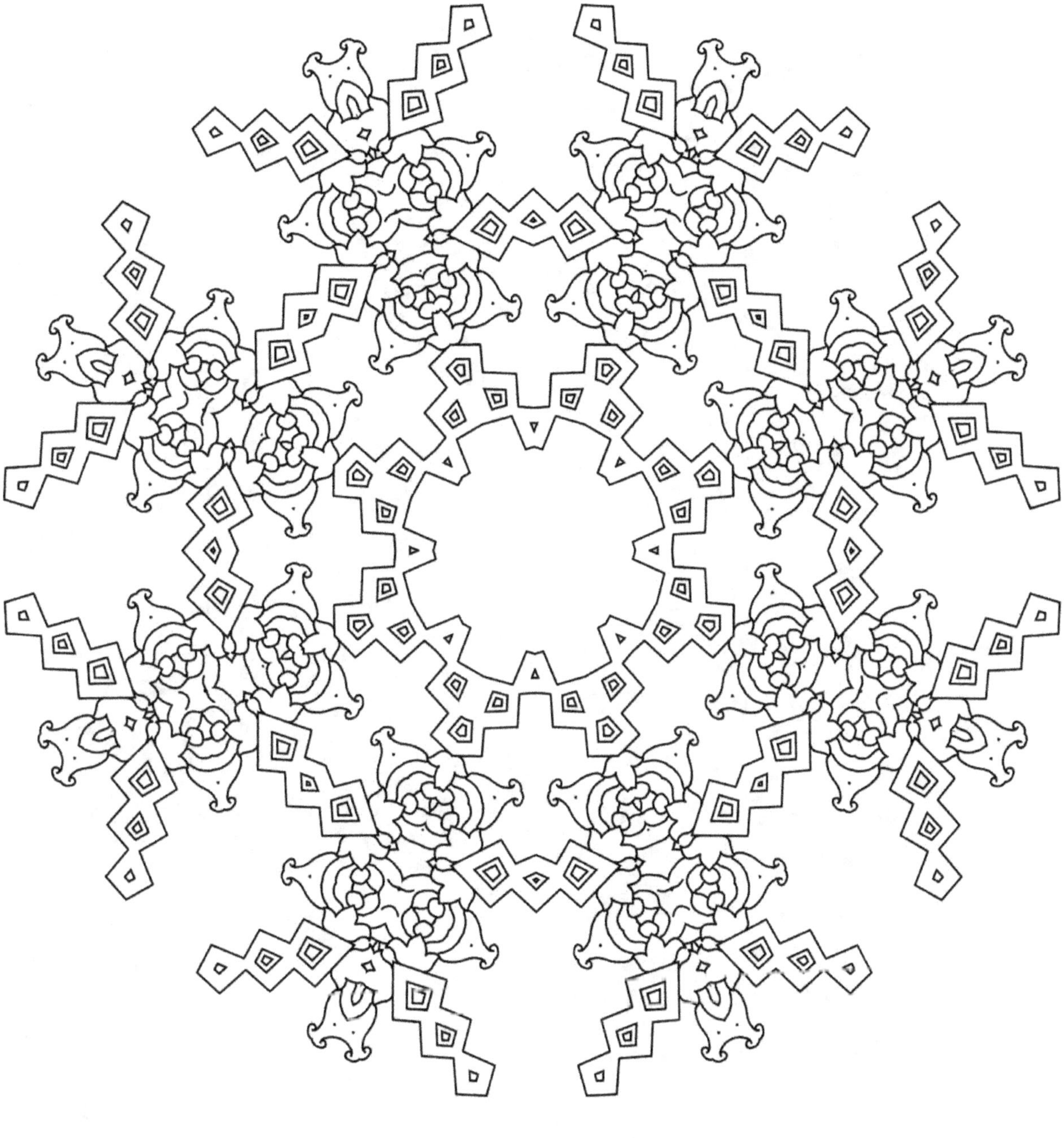

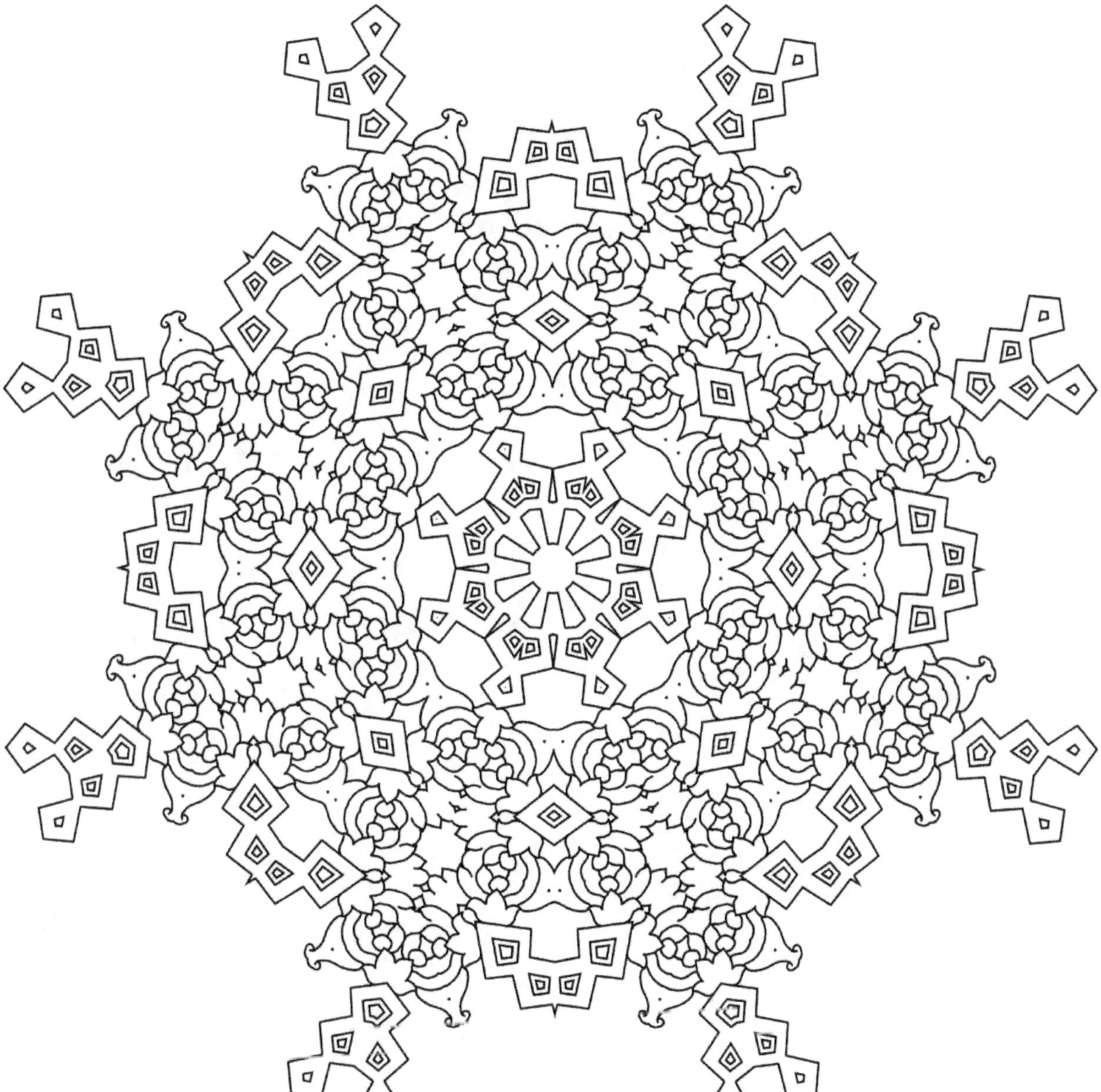

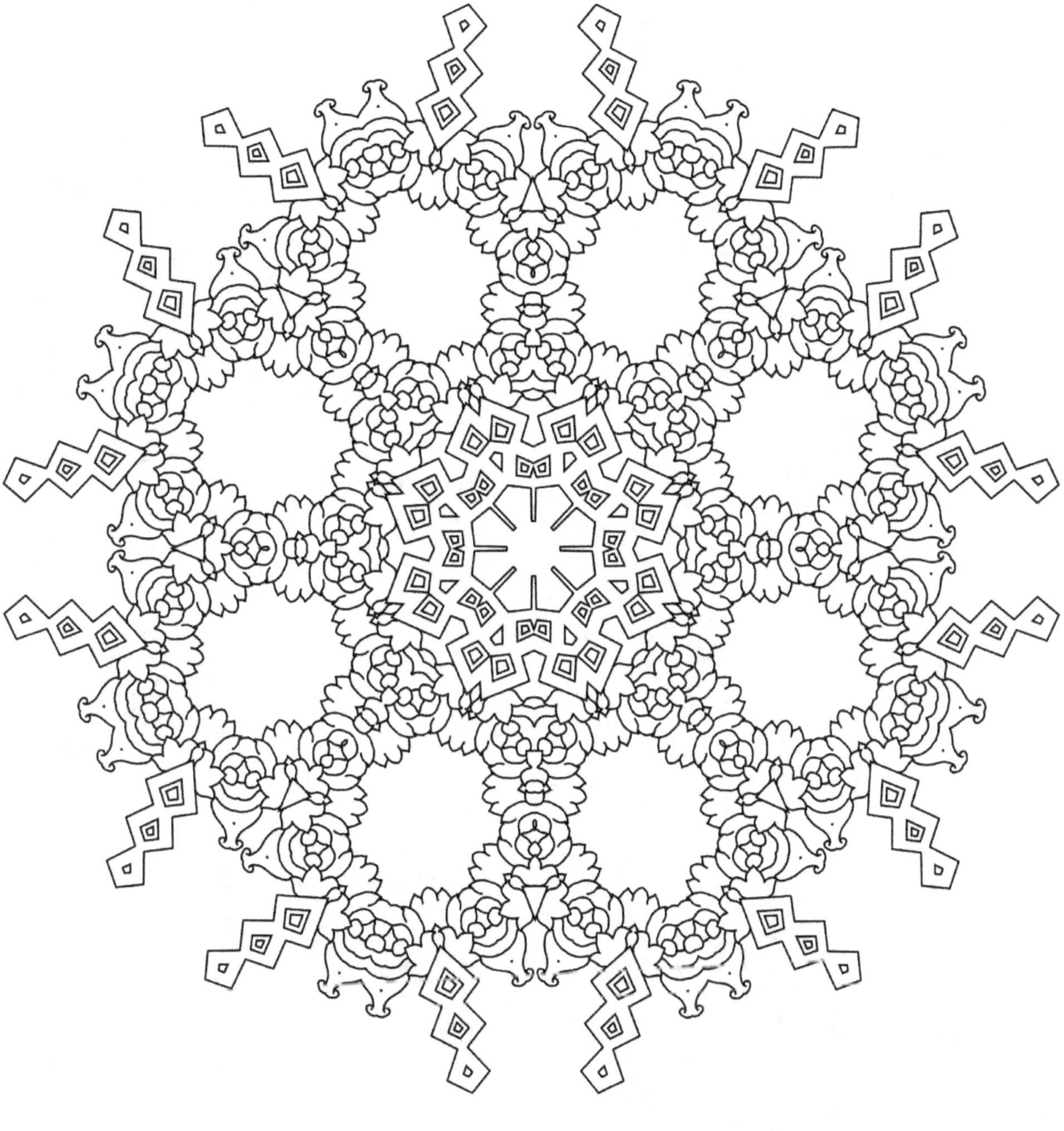

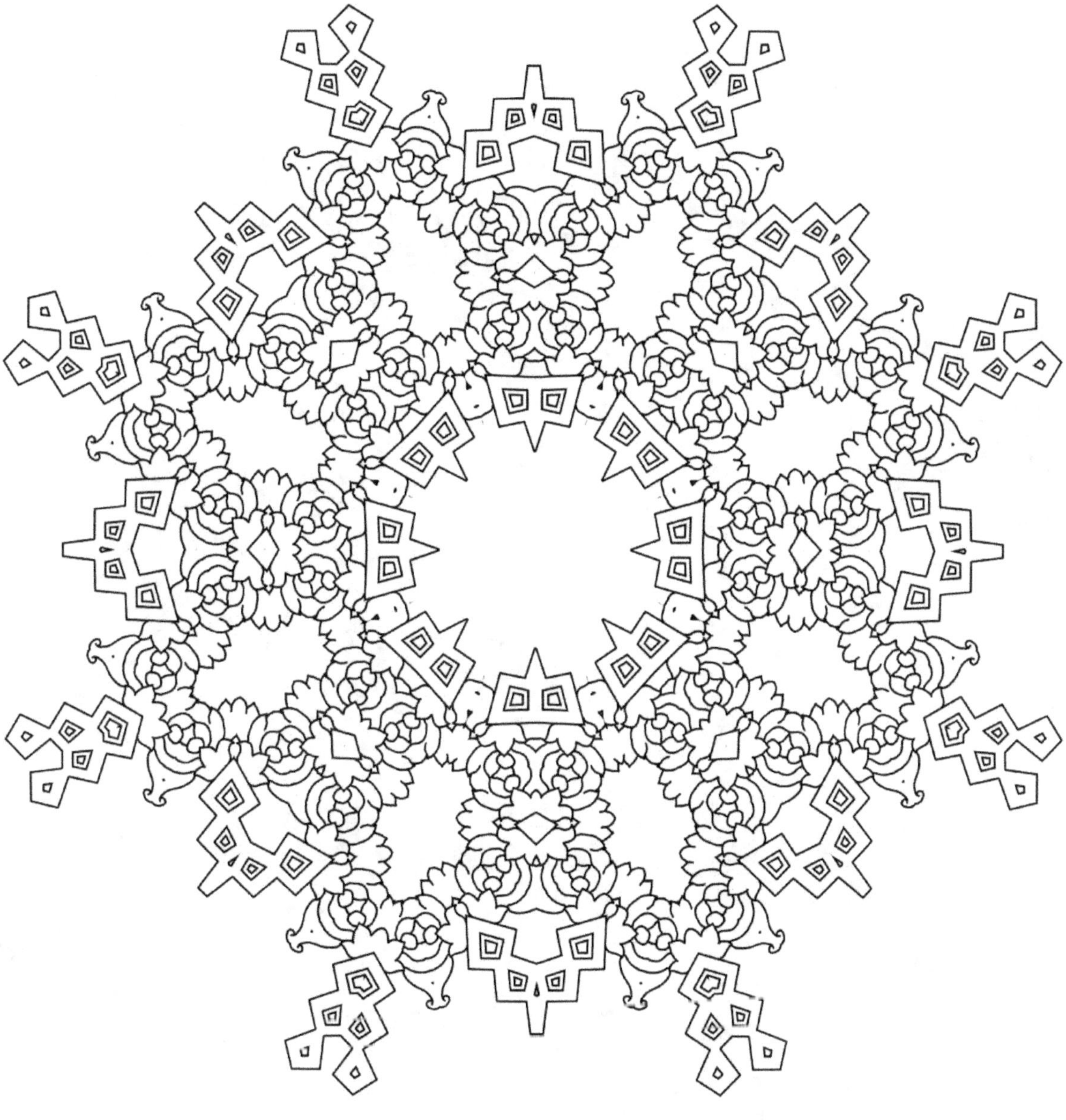

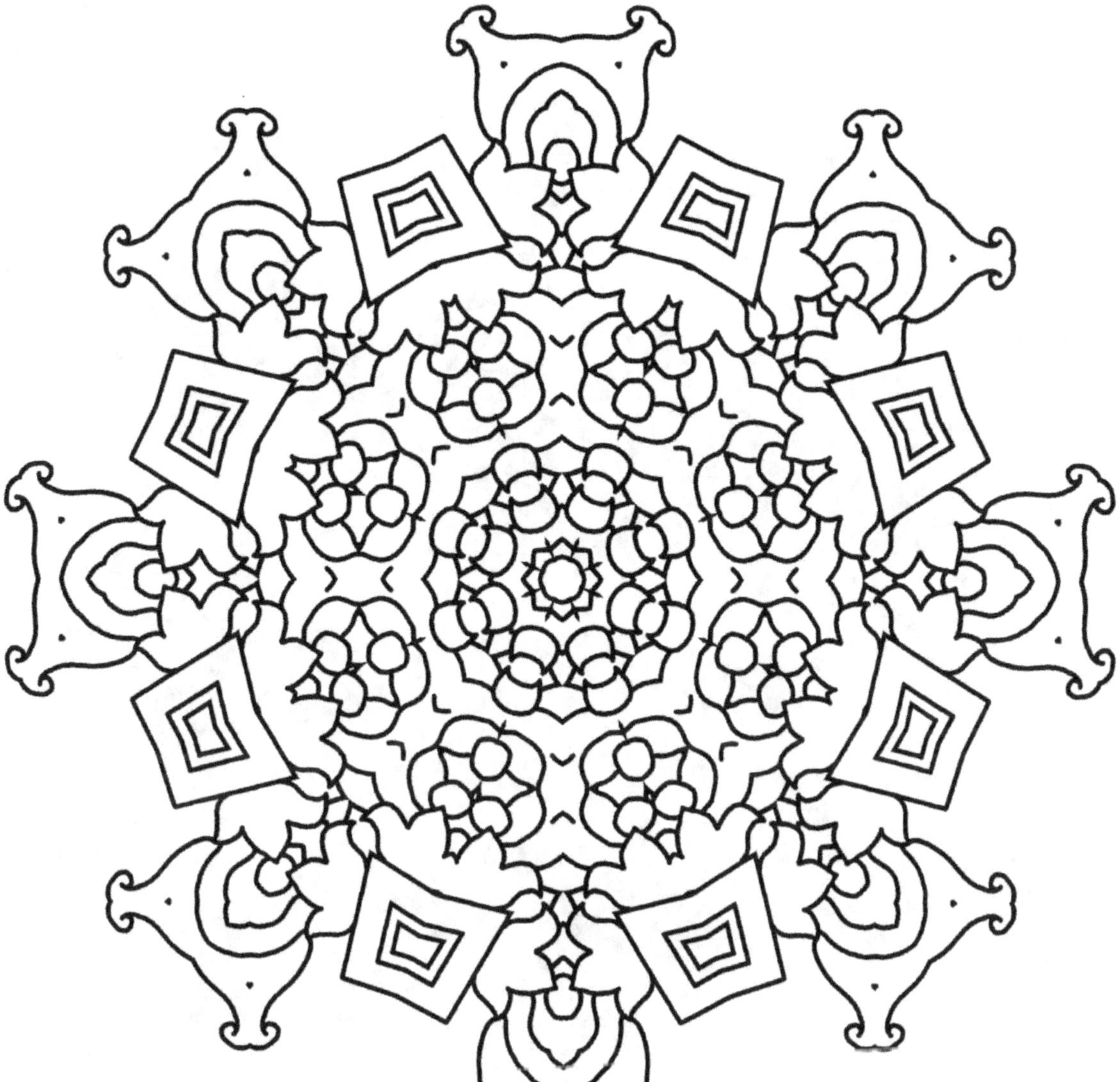

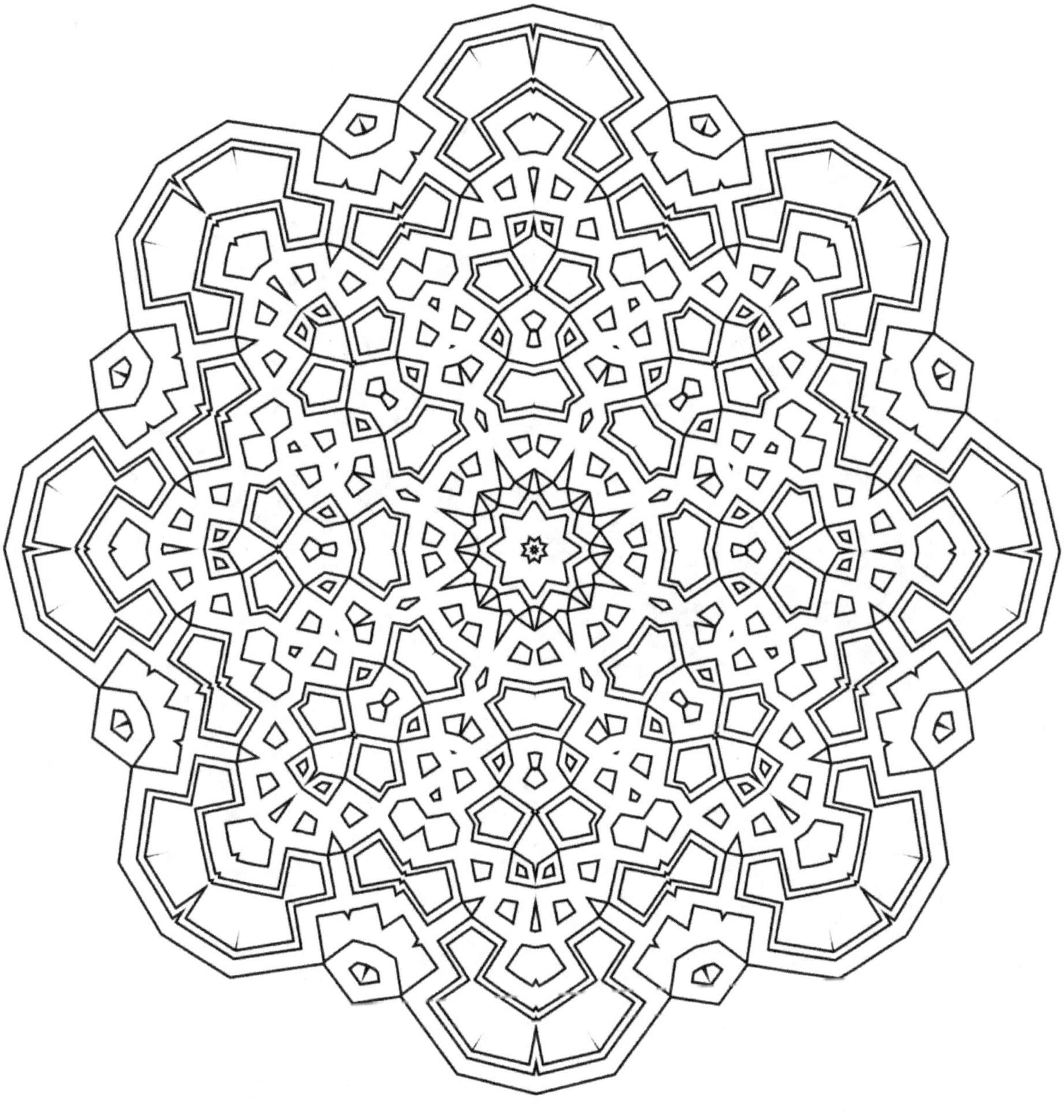

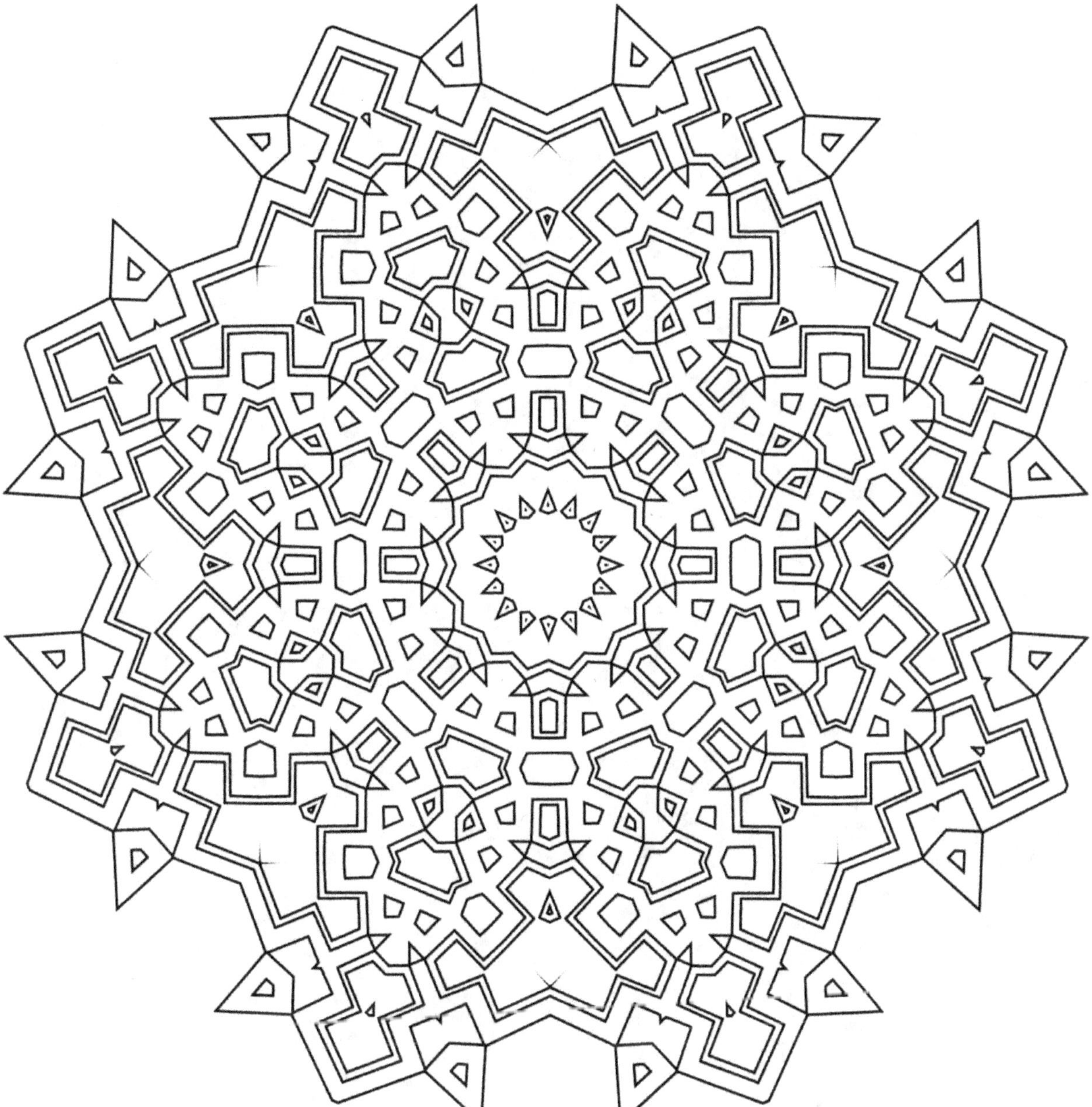

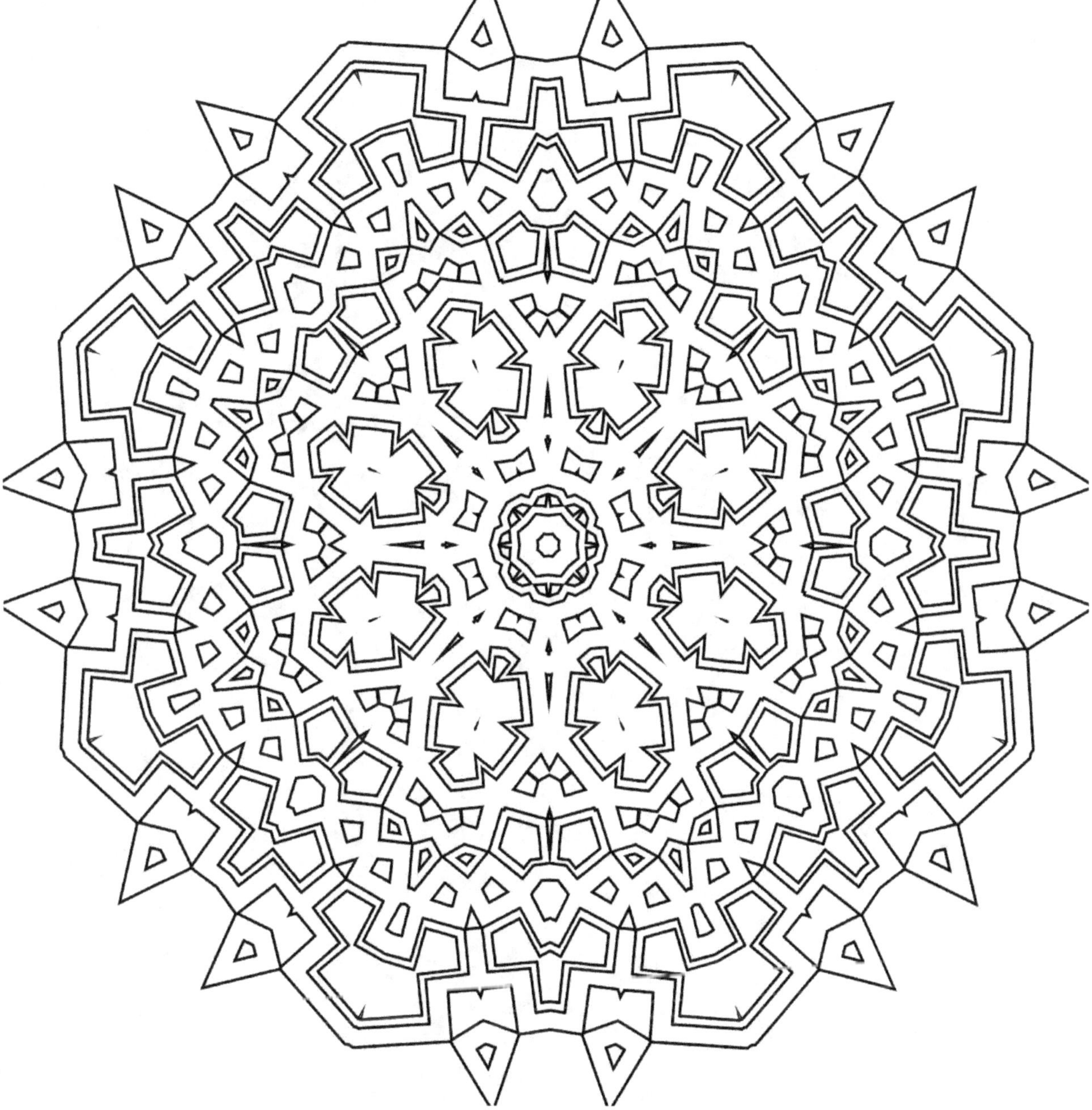

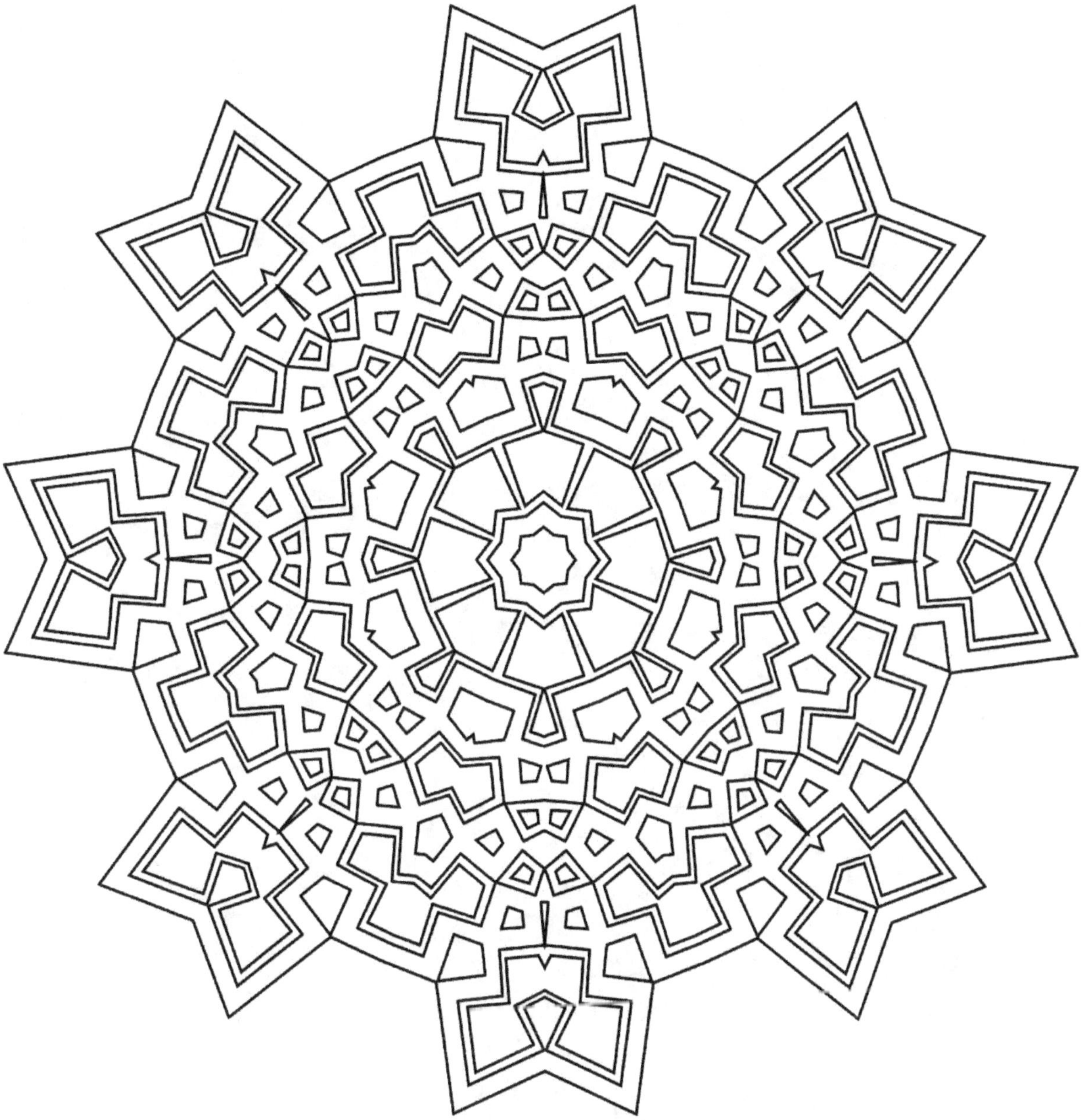

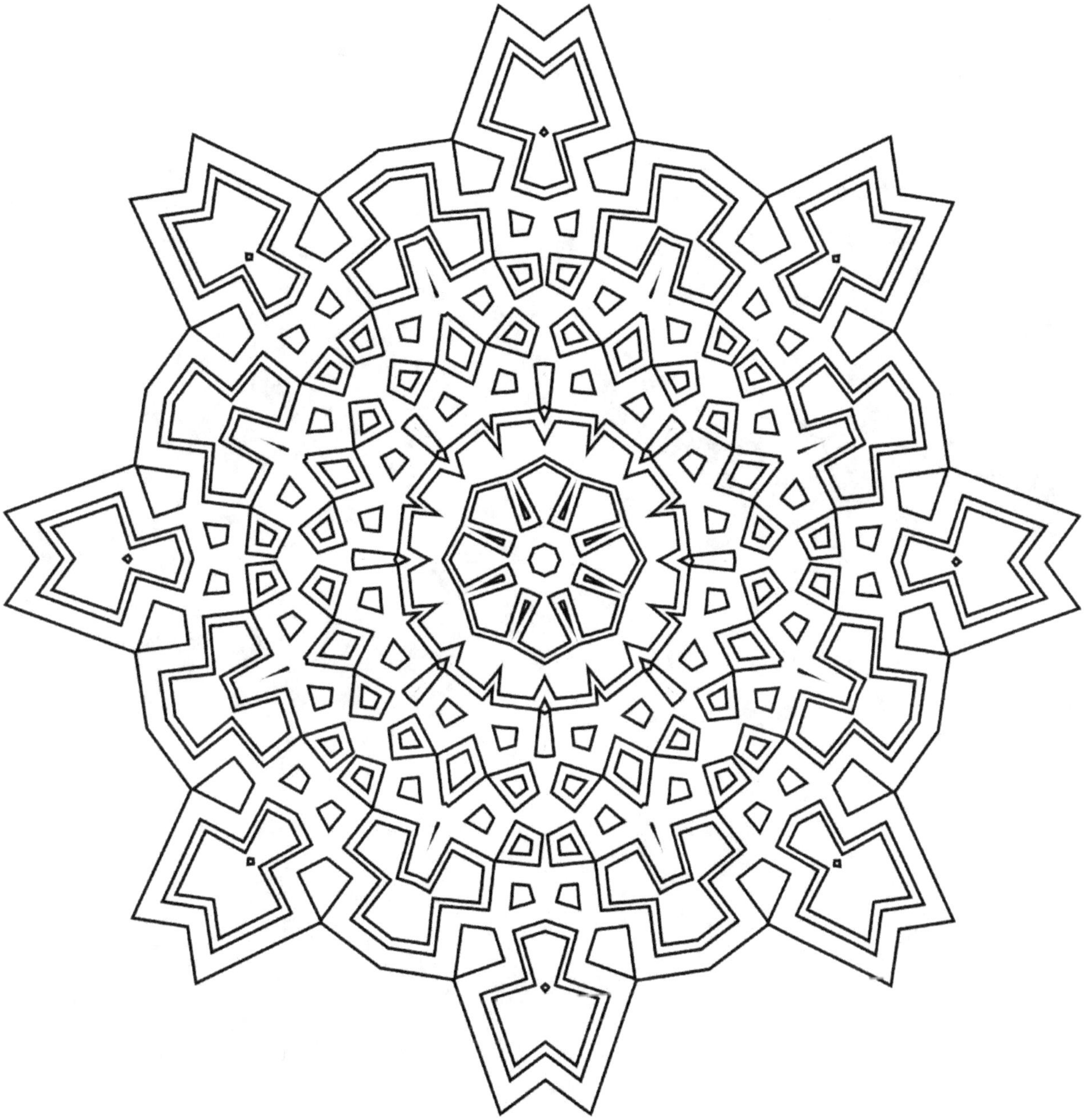

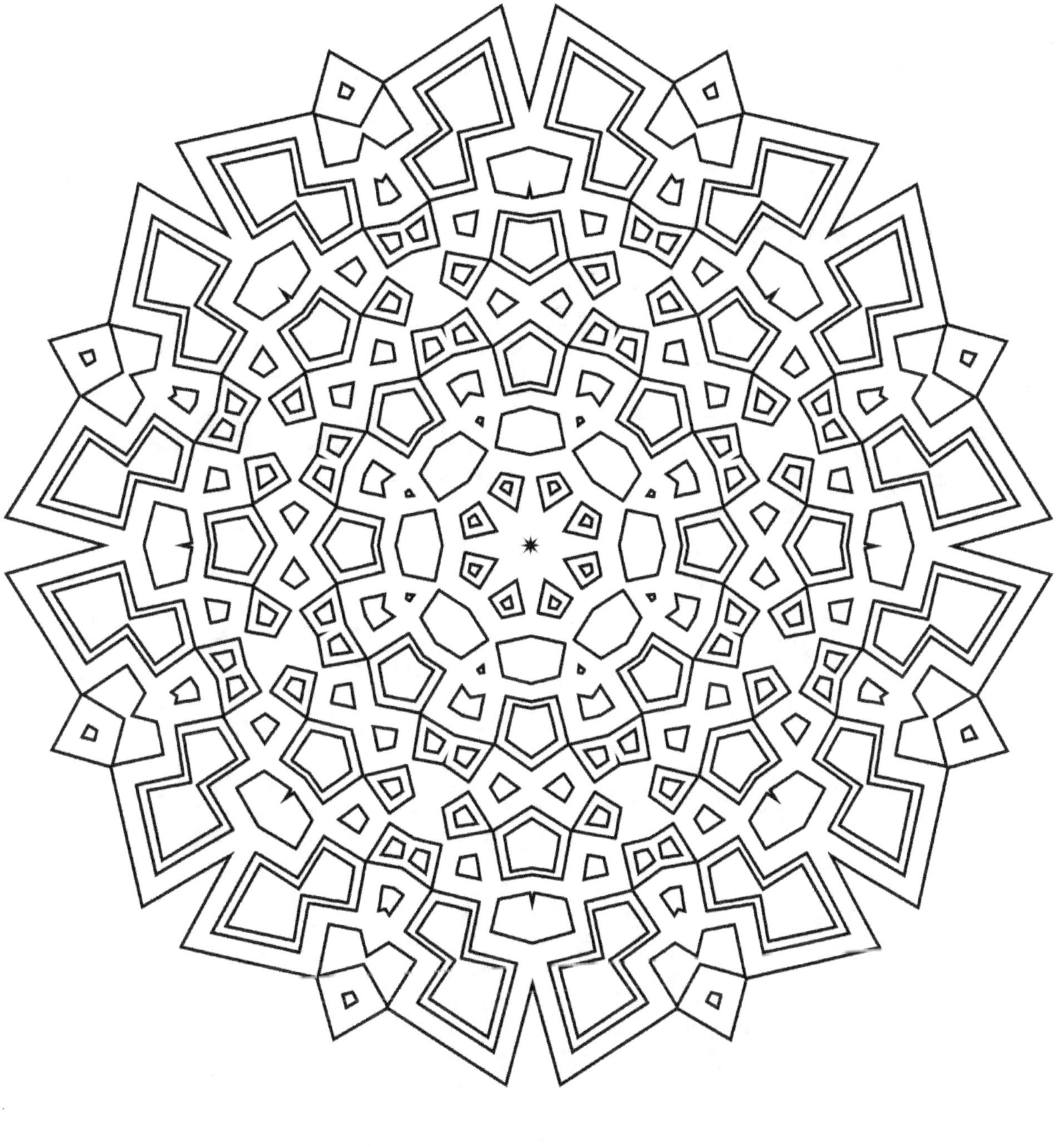

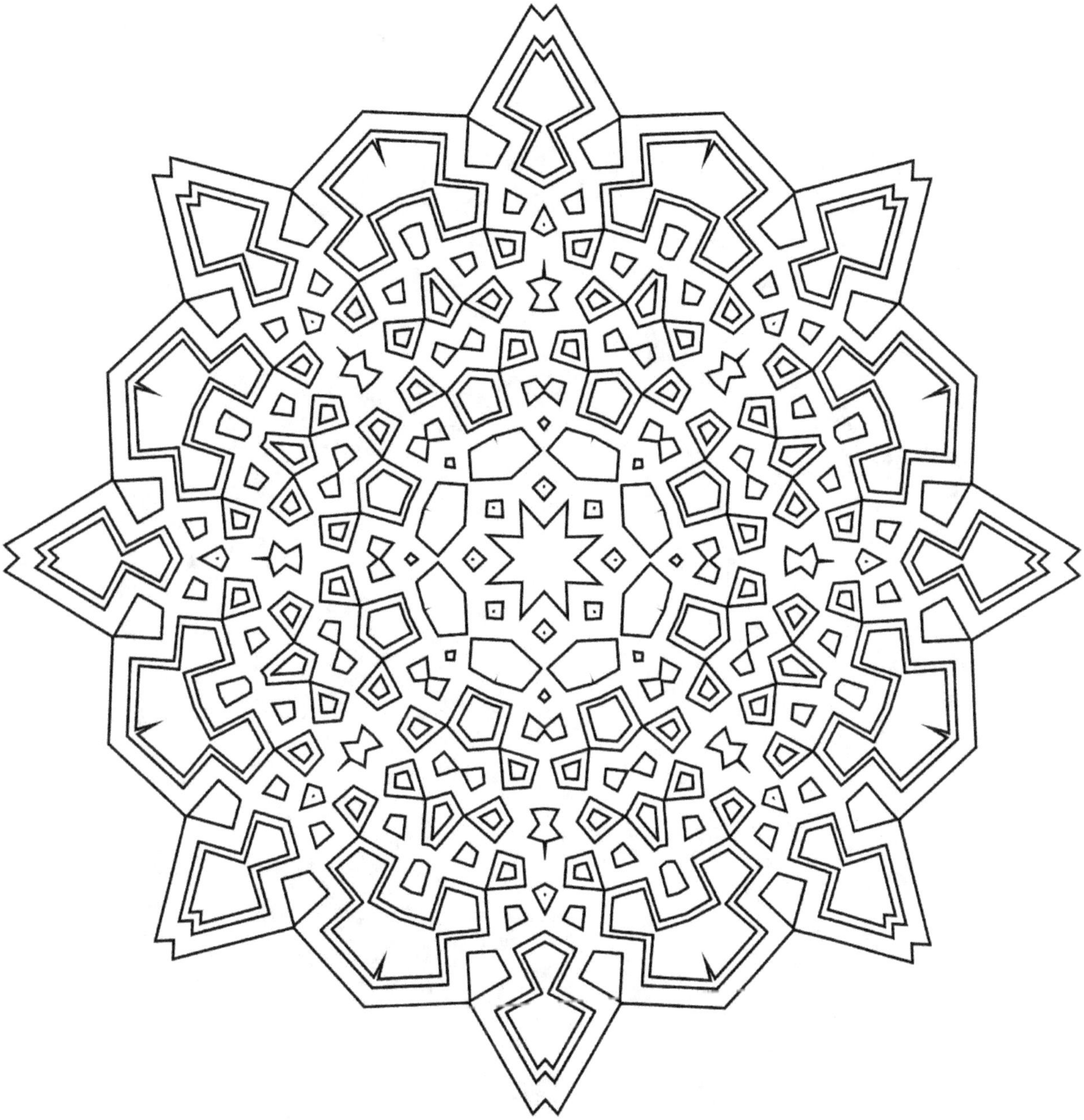

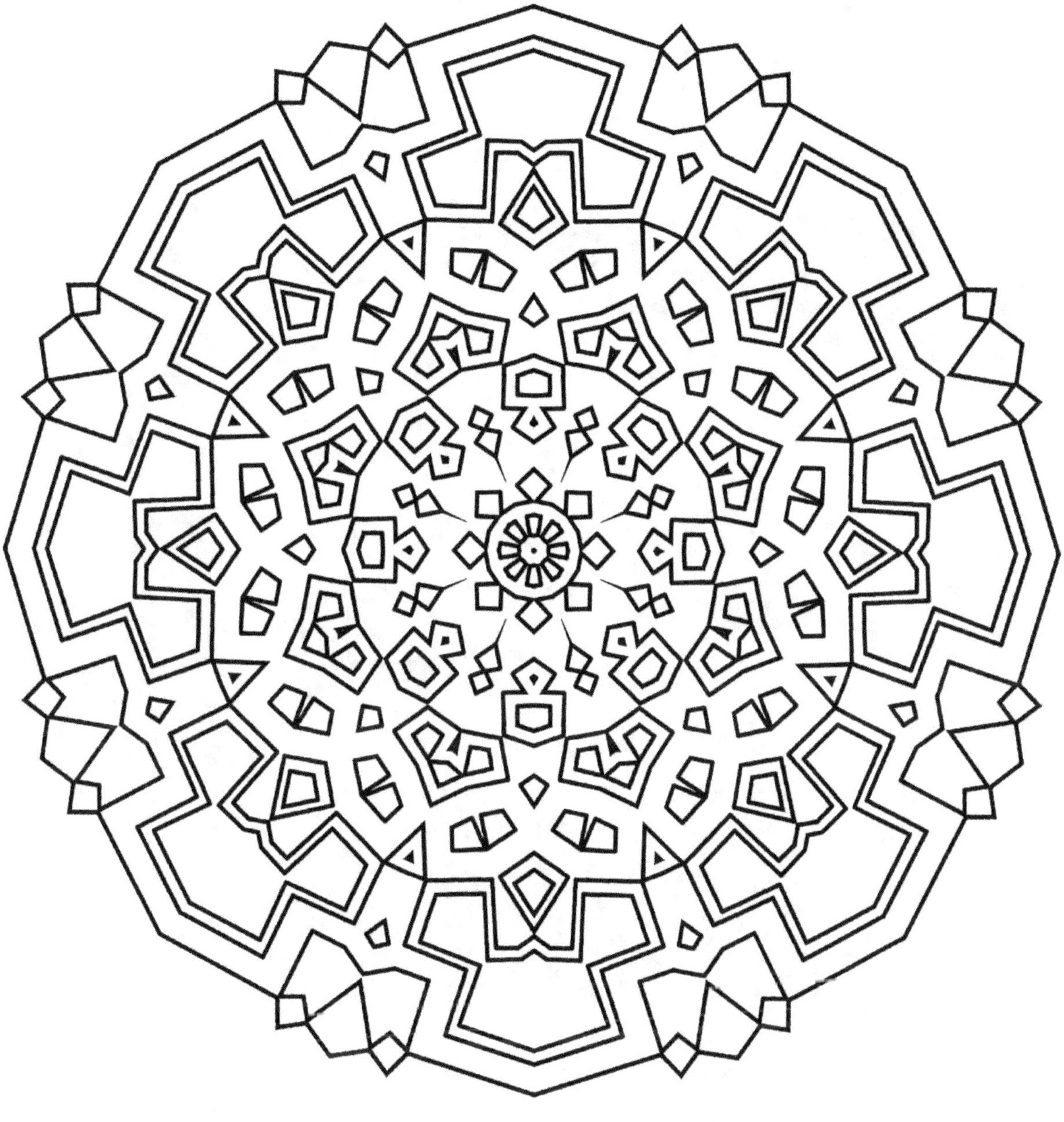

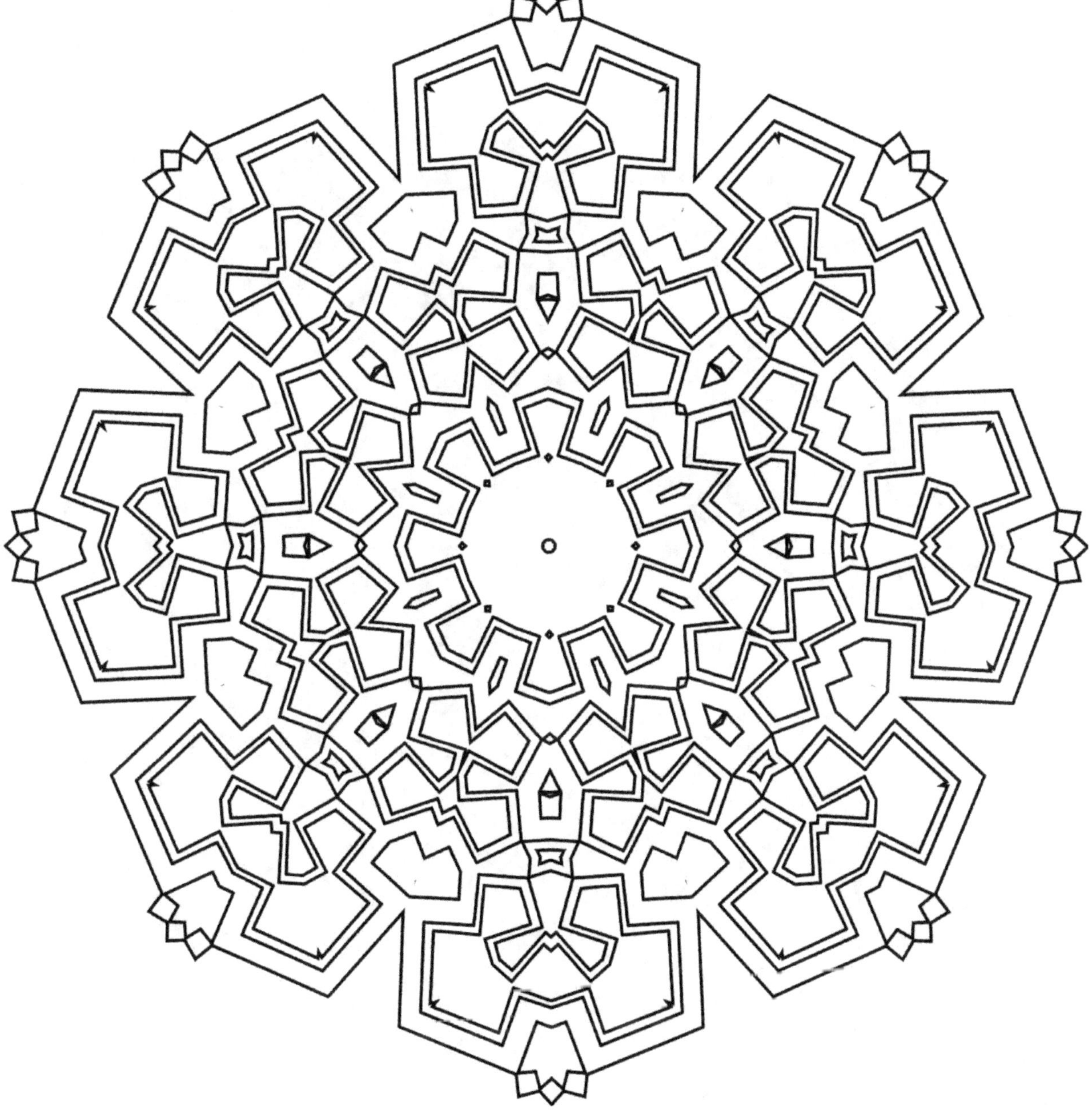

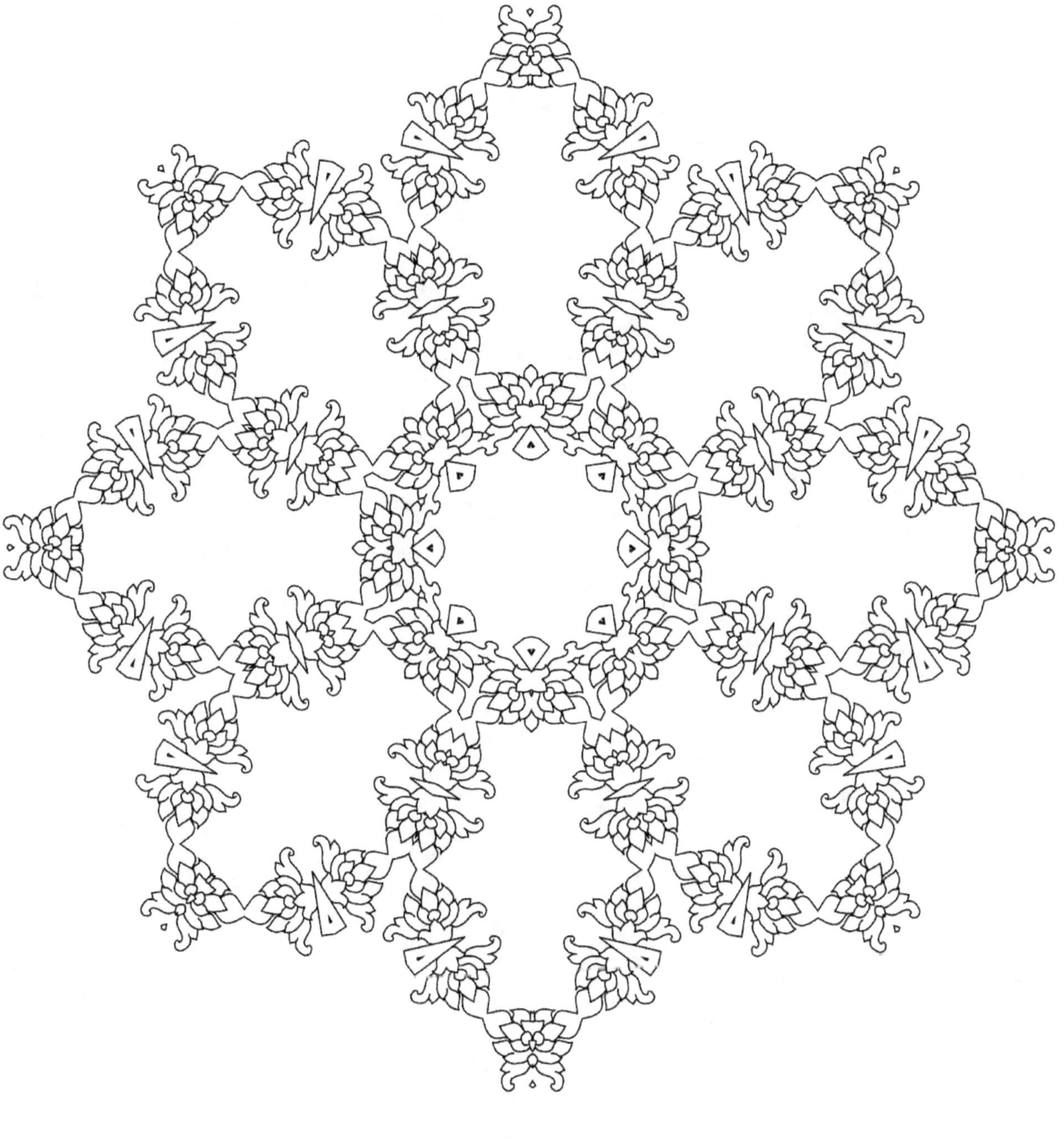

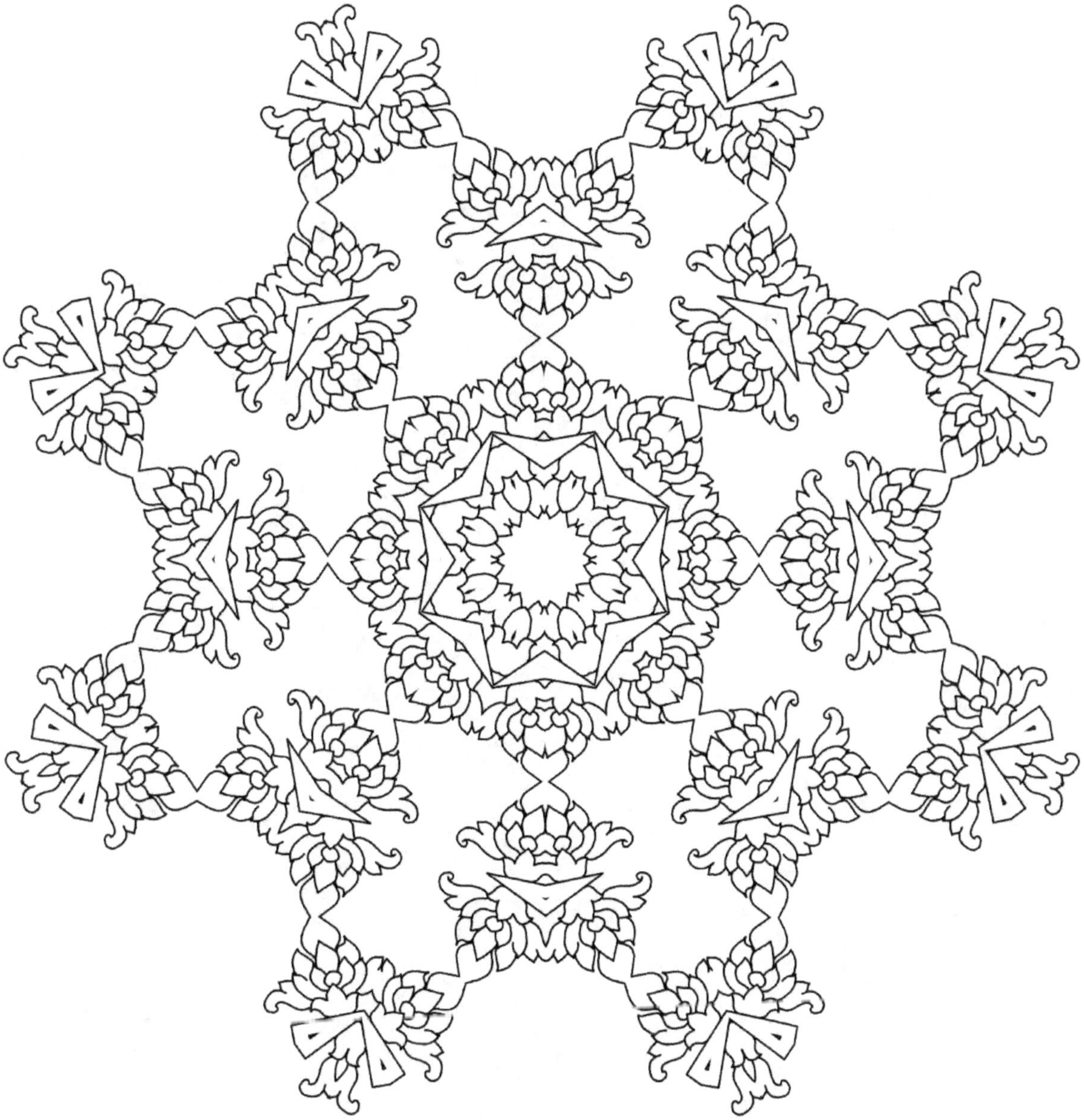

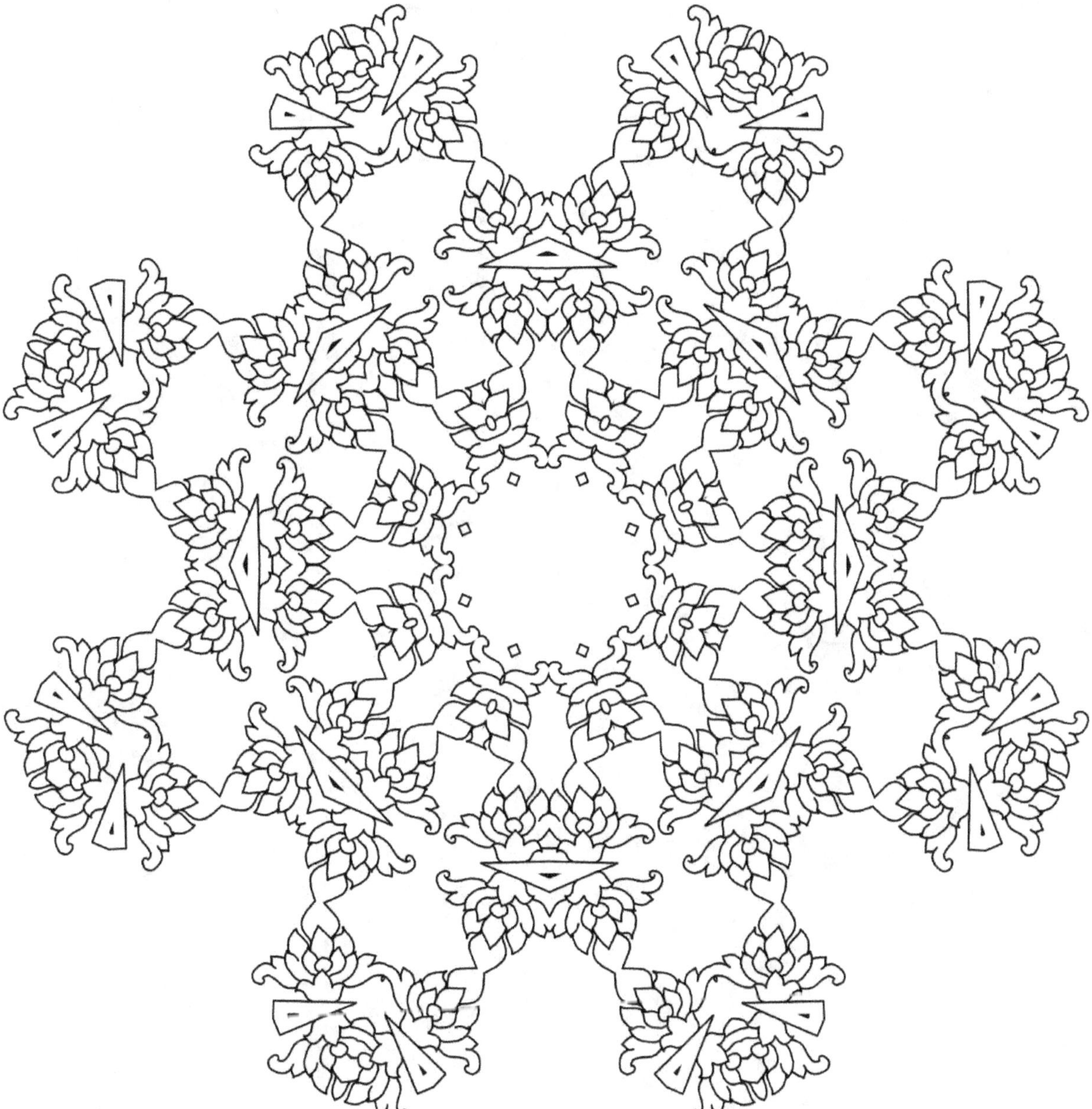

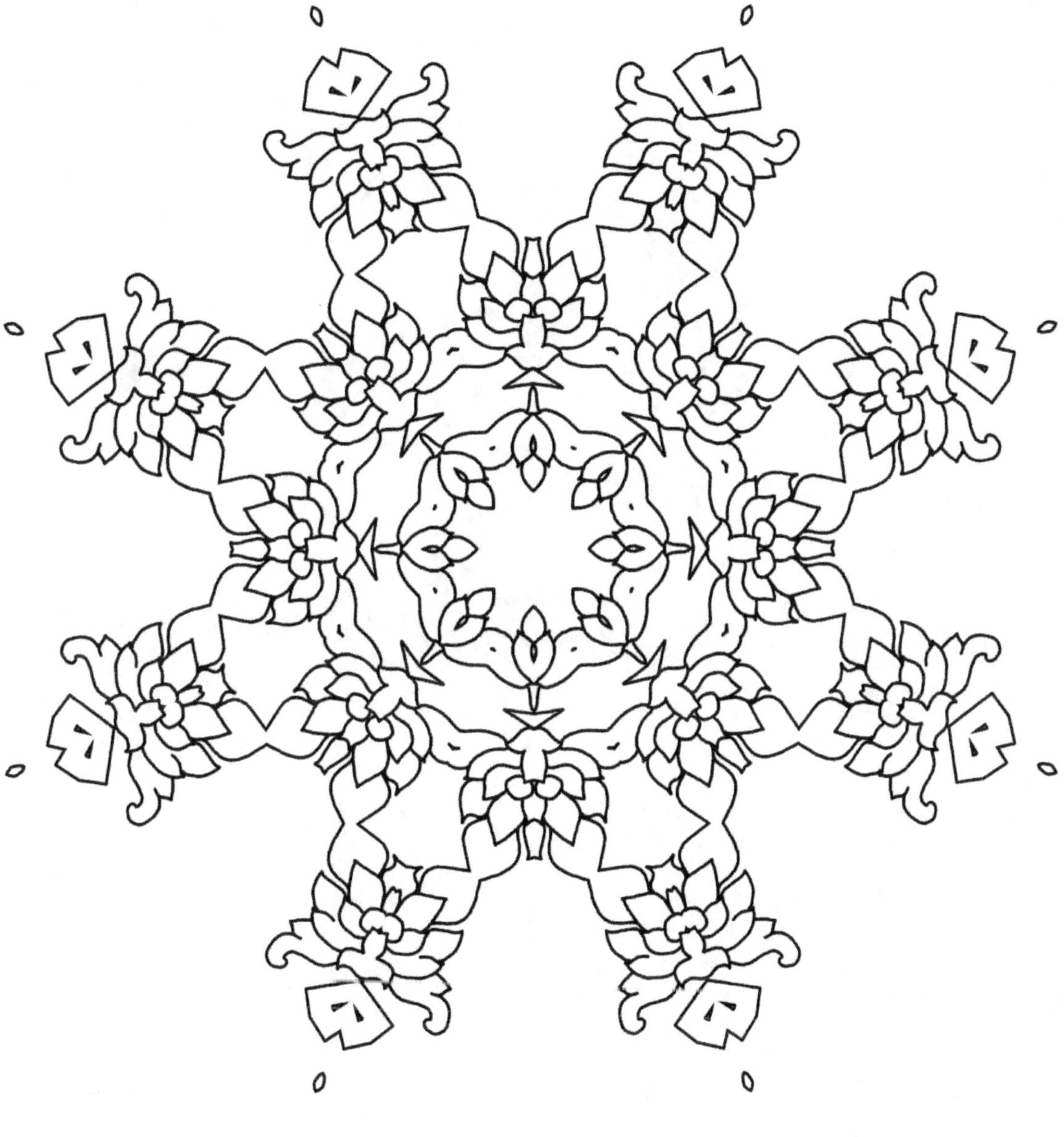

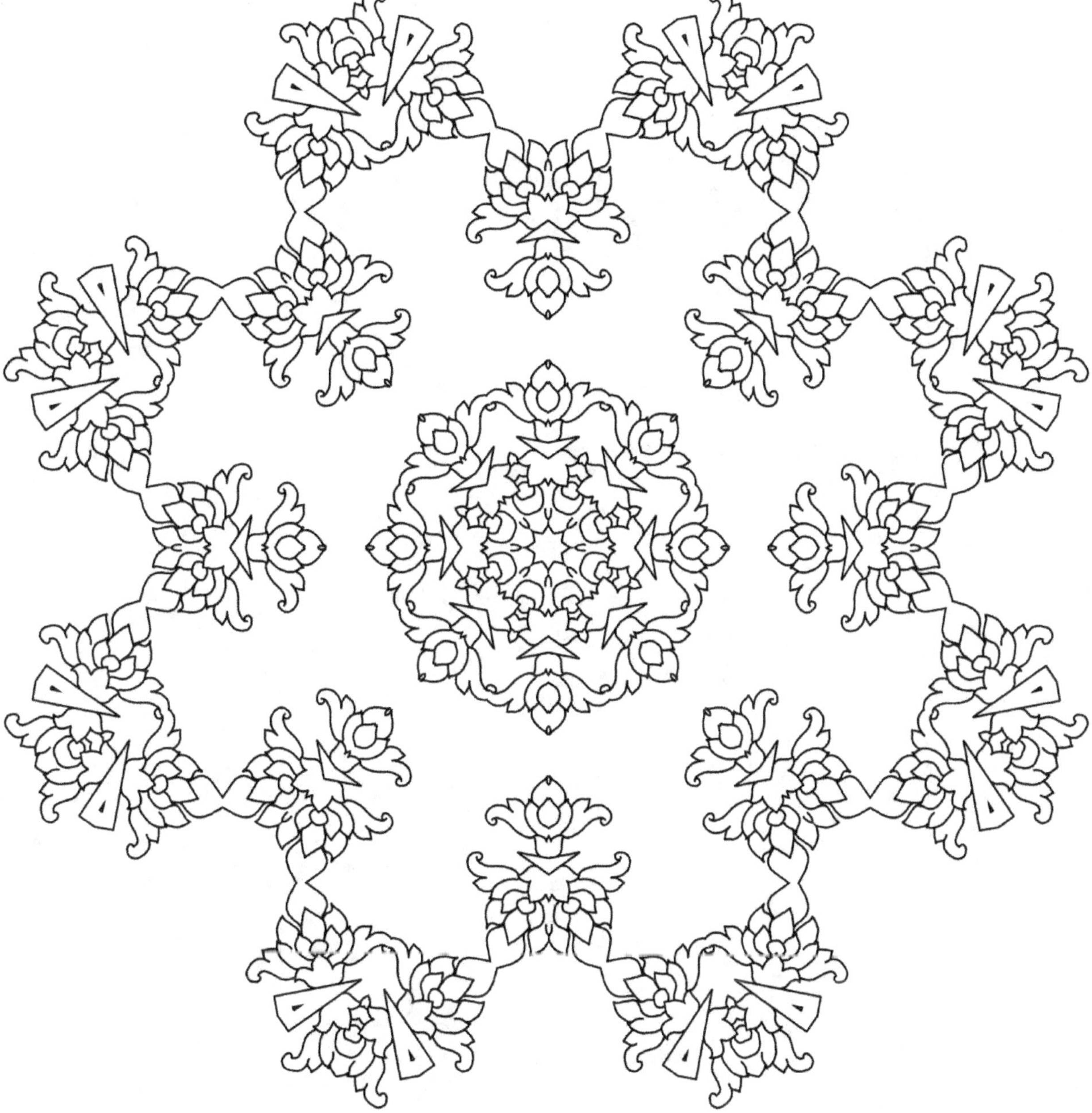

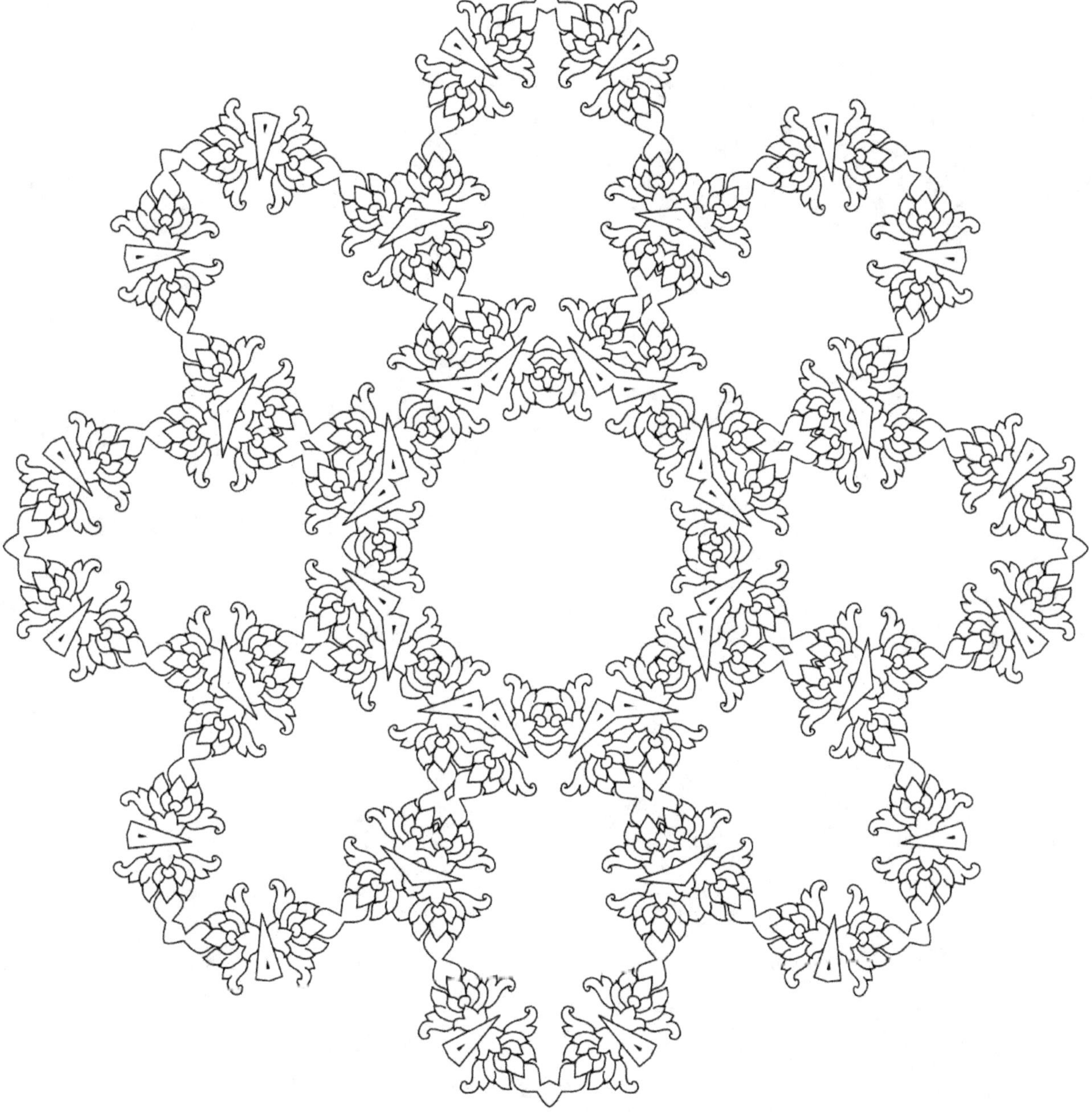

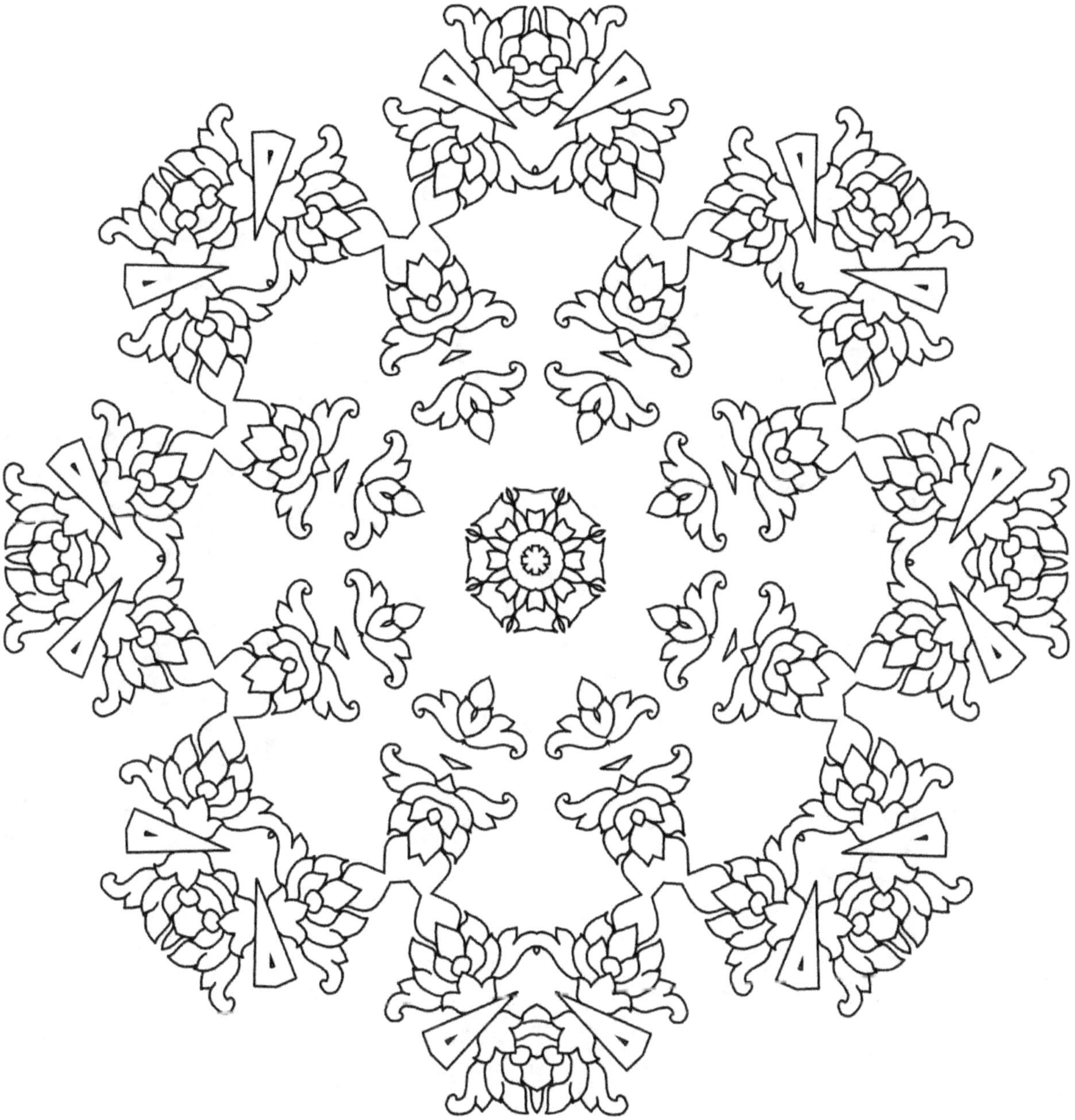

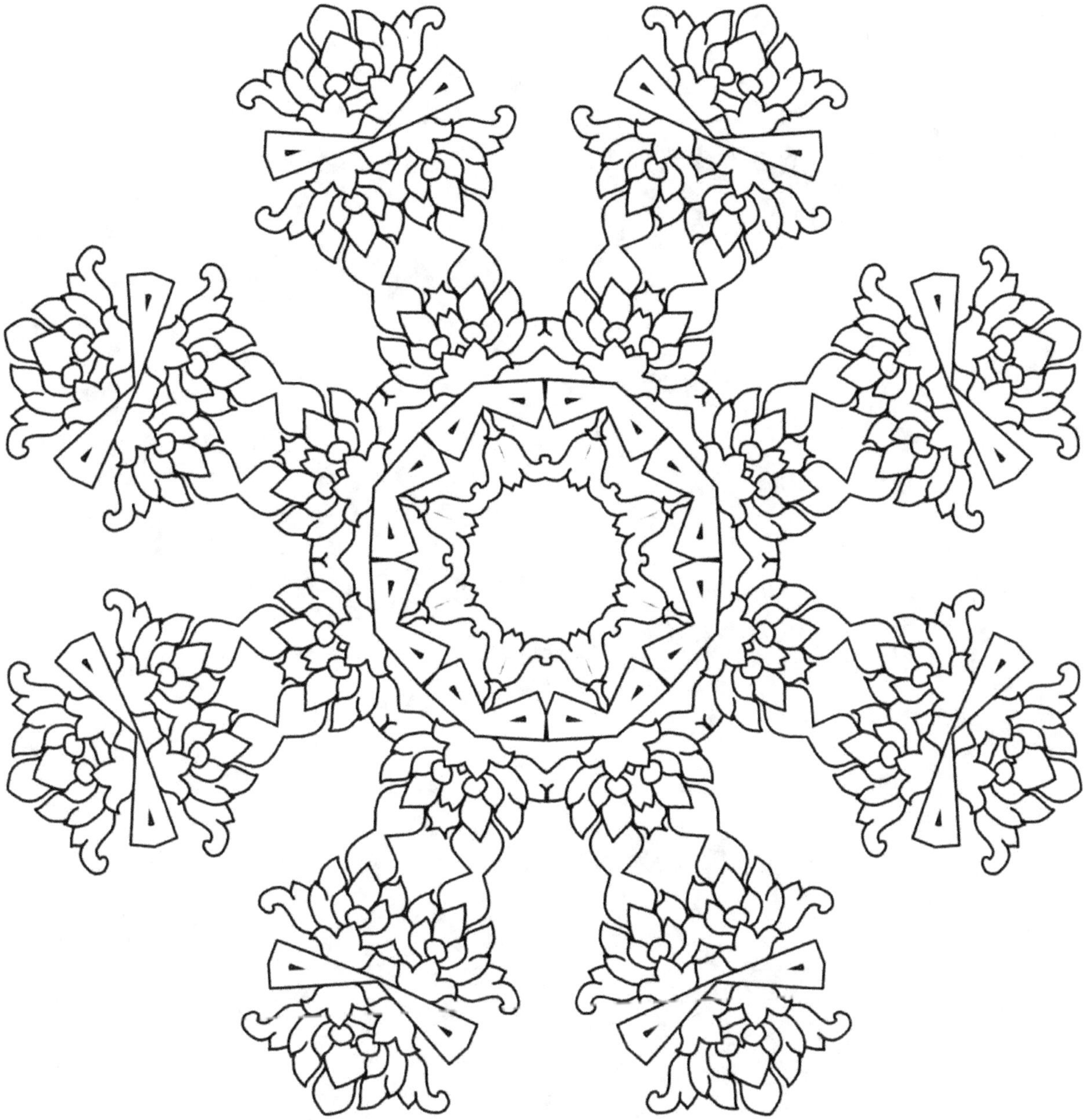

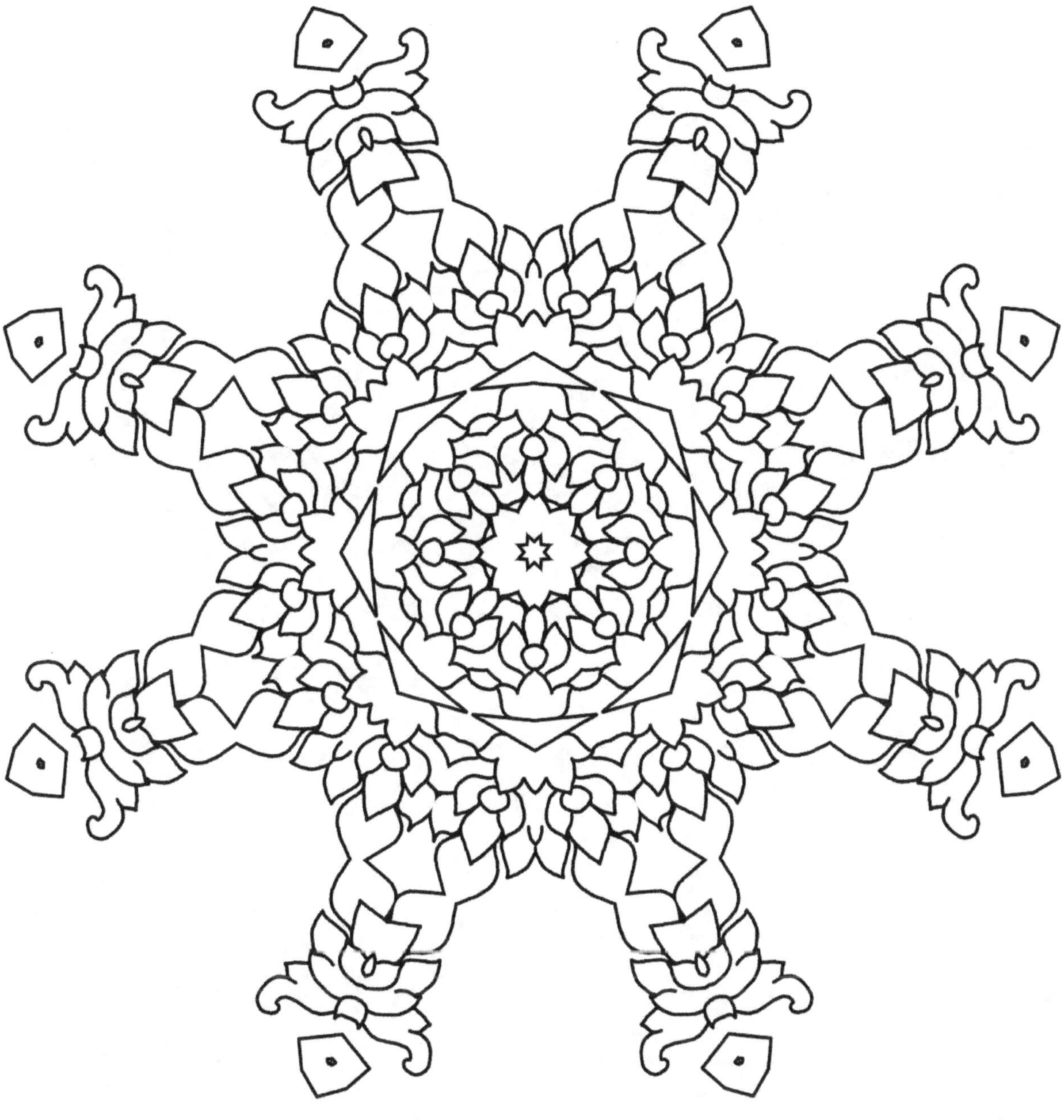

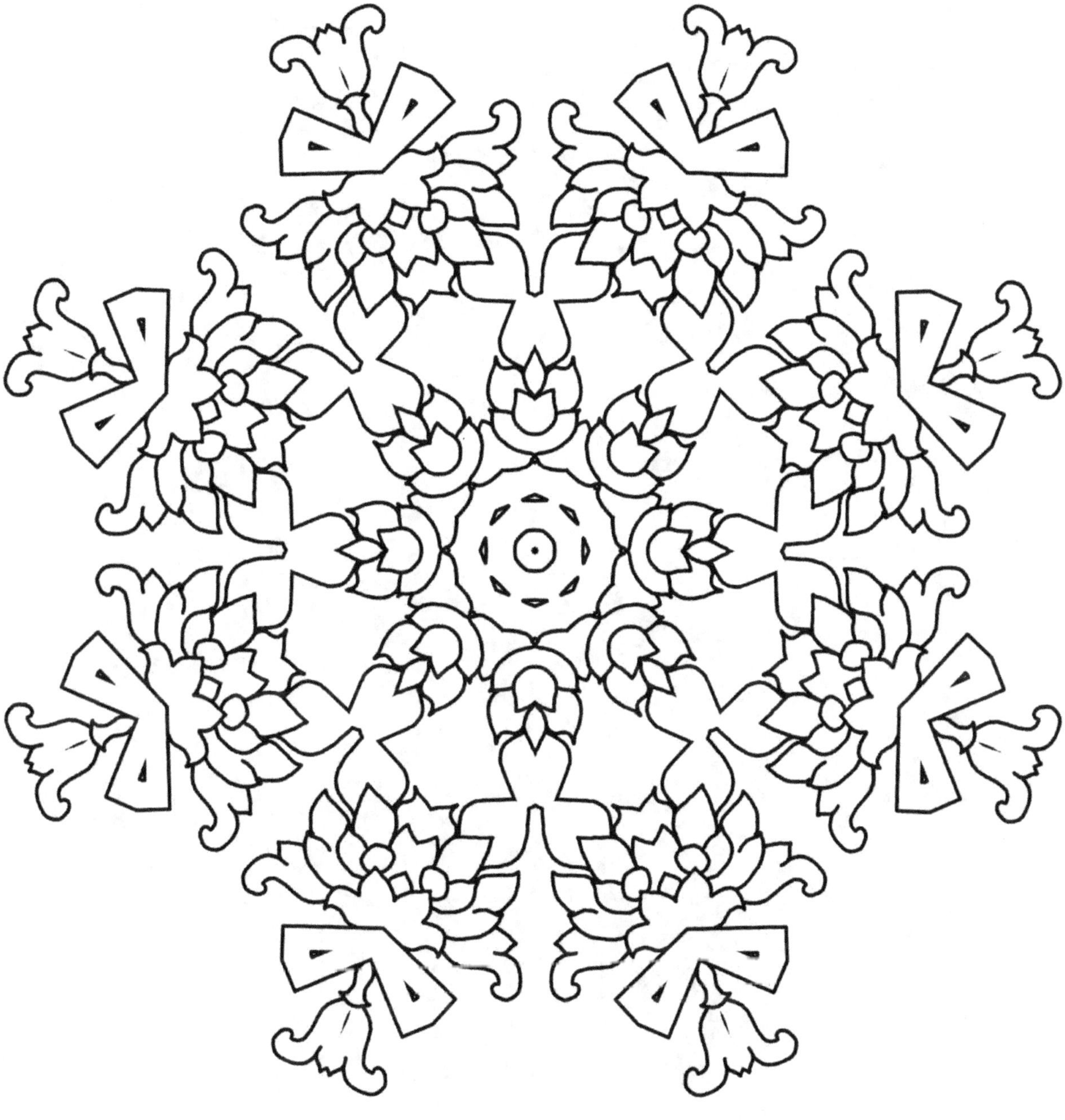

Thank you

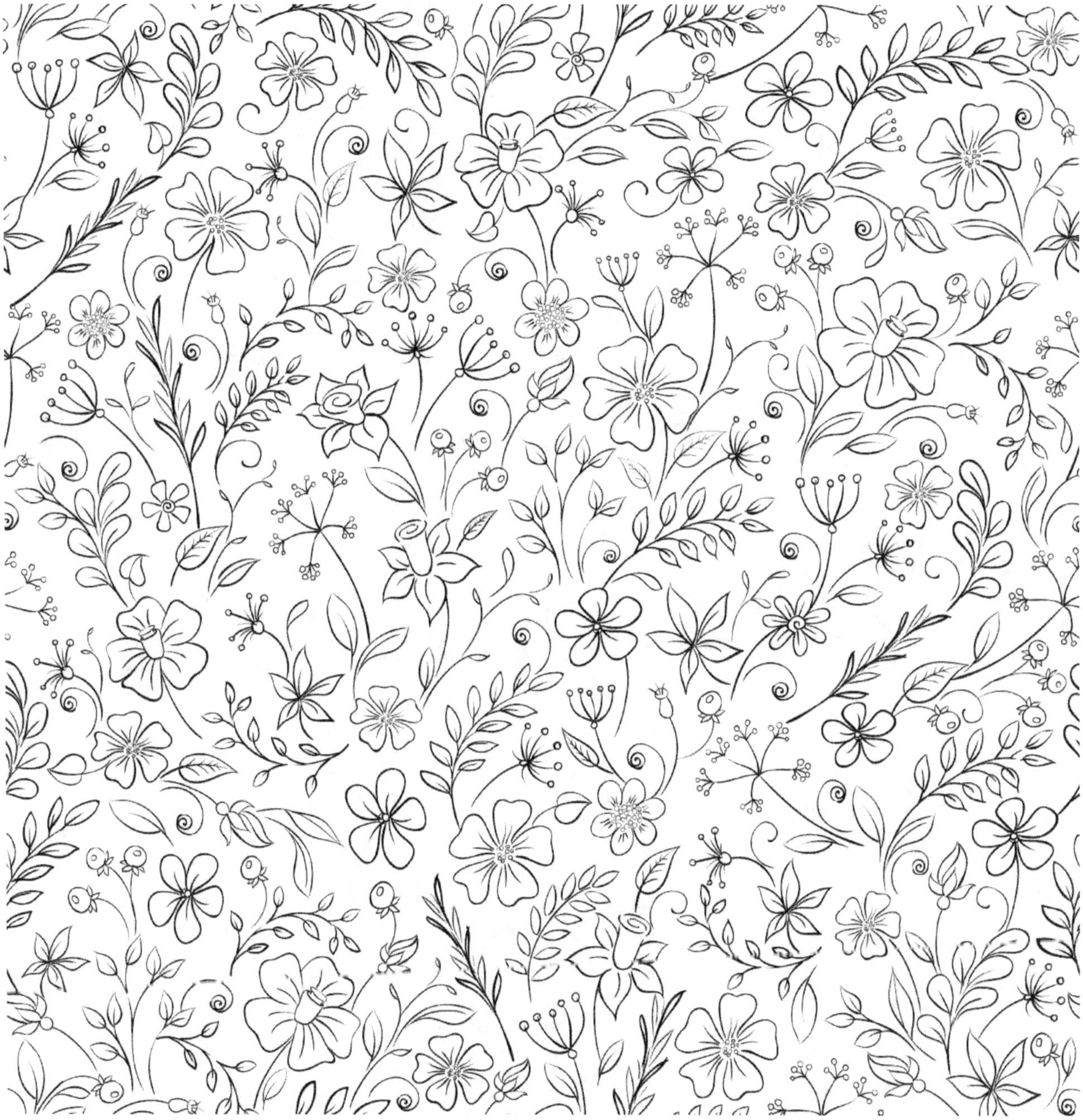

www.ingramcontent.com/pod-product-compliance
Lightning Source LLC
Chambersburg PA
CBHW081116180526
45170CB00008B/2867

Mandala
Free Spirit Coloring Book

Copyright: Published in the United States by Jacinta Schultz
Published December 2016
ISBN-13: 978-1541317093
ISBN-10: 1541317092